Swindon College

the design icon
of a generation

Mini

the design **icon** of a generation

Mini

Based on a text **by LJK Setright**
Foreword by **Sir Terence Conran**

Virgin

First published in Great Britain in 1999 by
Virgin Publishing Ltd
Thames Wharf Studios
Rainville Road
London W6 9HT

Copyright © 1999 Rover Group Ltd

Mini, Mini Cooper and the Mini Shape are trademarks of Rover Group Limited used under license by Virgin Publishing Limited.

Based on a text by LJK Setright.

A catalogue record for this book is available from the British Library.

ISBN 1 85227 815 3

Printed and bound in Great Britain by
Butler & Tanner Ltd, Frome and London

Artistic Concept and Art Direction:
Derek Forsyth/Blueprint
Design: Janet James. Victoria Fenton

Contents

Foreword	6
Upstart	11
Gamine	43
Workhorse	69
Racer	101
Film idol	143
Freak	159
Harbinger	193
Picture credits	222

Foreword

The Mini, as we all know, is a classic. Alec Issigonis' brilliant design was original, immediately appealing, quirky and looked unlike any car we'd seen before. (There have been quite a few pale imitations since, but it's still fair to say that the Mini remains one of a handful of cars that is instantly recognizable.)

One of the greatest achievements of the Mini – easy to overlook with hindsight – is that it anticipated the changing social values that would come to the fore in the 1960s, when the post-war baby boomers were looking to express their independence from previous generations through the fashions of Mary Quant and the music of The Beatles, the Stones and The Who. Along with the miniskirt, the Mini Cooper became an icon of British modernity. But unlike fashion and music, the Mini's appeal transcended not only class and sex, but age.

By being fun, the Mini made a virtue of its potential shortcomings, most notably the relatively cramped interior. 'How many people can you fit into a Mini?' was not just the basis for numerous jokes, but for newspaper and magazine articles with photographs of an improbable number of people stuffed into the car, limbs hanging out of windows and doors. The Mini represented independence

and spontaneity: you could park it anywhere (or just about) and turn it on a sixpence (or just about). The wit and character of the car transferred itself to the owner, and in films and on television it became shorthand for 'good guy' or 'party girl'. When a hapless, latter-day Robin Hood makes his getaway in a Mini, you're urging the car to accelerate as surely as you know the cops will catch up with him.

I don't think you can set out to design a classic for mass consumption: and I don't suppose that's what Issigonis set out to do. Of course, a team of people was involved in creating the Mini – the car's rubber suspension was designed by Alex Moulton who later designed a foldaway bicycle and went on to found a company making beautiful bespoke bicycles. But the vision for the Mini was that of one man, Alec Issigonis, and that, I would argue, is why it has character and warmth. Interestingly, in the same year that the Mini was launched, another car manufacturer launched a family car called the Edsel. The Mini was designed around Issigonis' intelligence, conviction, and the gut feeling that he was on to something good; the Edsel, by contrast, was shaped by incredibly detailed market research and focus groups about exactly (or supposedly) what consumers wanted. Whilst I am not suggesting in any way that the two cars were in competition, I think it is telling that the Edsel was a spectacular failure.

Forty years on, the Mini still looks fresh and fun. For many people, the Mini was, or will be, the first car that they own. However many cars they subsequently get through, I doubt that they will be remembered with the same care and affection as their Mini. It's a classy little classless car, and I wish it very many more happy birthdays.

Sir Terence Conran

Thank you, Sir Alec Issigonis...

John Cooper
racer/engineer

iconoclastic
ingenious
intriguing
Upstart

'I arrived at the dimensions of the doorpockets quite simply, by calculating the volume of the ingredients for the ideal Dry Martini cocktail: one bottle of Vermouth, and 27 bottles of gin!' He was joking. It was a favourite pastime of Sir Alec Issigonis, and there were many enquirers (especially members of the press) who left feeling slightly dazed and not sure whether to believe the outrageous things that he had just said. Did he really make the seats so uncomfortable because he believed in people being kept alert at the wheel? Did he really dislike radio so much that he made no provision for it in the car?

It was to me that he made the joke about the volume of the doorpockets. But we understood each other pretty well and he knew that I knew that he was not being serious. It needed no calculation, just a practised eye (and the practising could be done equally well with a Mini or with a Martini), to see that he had calculated nothing of the sort.

Left There was talk about the doorpockets, but the rear was pocketed too

Left 40 years young

We did not have calculators in our pockets in the 1950s: children were still being taught mental arithmetic. We had no personal computers. Digital processing was as yet unknown except to a handful of remote scientists; the reign of the logarithm had not yet ended. Engineers, when they did their calculations, used logarithmic slide rules. Good engineers knew that the validity of their basic concepts was what mattered, and they resorted to number-crunching only in order to check the accuracy of their inspiration. In this and in other respects, Issigonis was a good engineer.

If we had no computers in those pre-Mini days, we also had to manage (how did we ever do it?) without many other things. A world war had given us the spirit to endure want; but, exhausted of that spirit after the war was over, we grew depressed and resentful in the years of ensuing austerity. The rationing that had begun in Britain

early in 1940 did not end until 1954, but already some things were beginning to improve: unemployment in Britain, never less than 10% between the wars and as high as 20% in 1932, was now down to about 2%, and, if wages were not uniformly good (least of all for women, who were forming an increasing proportion of the labour force), at least the wheels were going round, and the money was beginning to do likewise.

We were, in short, working our way up out of our miserable situation. Back in 1951, only 62% of British dwellings had a bathroom or shower, only 80% had their own toilet and scarcely any had central heating; but the deficits were halved in little more than a decade. In 1951 hardly one household in fifteen had a television set; by 1955 the proportion had rocketed to one in four, the outstanding impetus being the coronation of Queen Elizabeth in 1953. Other luxuries, too, were becoming necessities – there was almost as steep a rise in telephones, vacuum cleaners, refrigerators and washing machines – but the one item above all others that was seen as the supreme symbol of the new consumer society was the motor car.

Below TV in 1950

Left The Coronation of Queen Elizabeth in 1953

Above British queues, as here in 1946, behaved nicely

Above A 1936 HRG
powered by a 1.5 litre
Meadows engine

In 1938 there had been one car to every 24
Britons, but the attrition of the war years had
brought this down to one for every 32 in 1945.
Production was greedily resumed as soon as
possible after the war, but the greater part of the
cars built were earmarked for export, in an effort
to earn precious dollars. It was not only middle-
class vanity which prompted the preference for
sizeable cars: our most important export markets
were not in the least interested in the little cars
that had been such a feature of the growing
mobility of the 1930s' population. Austin,
however much their reputation was supported by
memories of the tiny and tremendously
important Austin Seven of 1922 and after,
did not have any kind of baby car in
production in the early post-war years.

Such cars as were being made are, in retrospect,
almost embarrassing. There were few exceptions:
the Bristol was supreme in build, engineering and
roadgoing qualities; the Rolls-Royce (and its
badge-engineered brother Bentley) came close in
build quality, if remaining smugly retrograde in
other respects; HRG made a costly and beautifully
wrought little sports car of a type that should have
been considered obsolescent in 1936; and Riley
did their best to create a stylish modern car based
on old existing ironwork. For the rest, they were
narrow, high, heavy, soggy horrors that larded the
lean earth with the oil sweated from every engine
and transmission joint, swilled more petrol than
their performance justified, and were put together
so perfunctorily that it was doubtful whether they
would be worn out before they fell apart.

Tradition was dying, but it was dying hard.
People were very reluctant to abandon the myth
that a long bonnet signified power, an idea that
the car had inherited from the steam locomotive
with its long boiler. They believed that a high
bonnet signified authority. The long, high
bonnets of pre-war cars demanded a very high
driving position if you were to see where the car
was going. Seeing where it had come from
mattered little in the absence of serious traffic:
the rear window could be kept small for privacy
and (since glass is heavy and costly) for
cheapness. In short, the car was then not merely
a convenient means of getting about or even
of getting away: it was something that not only
reflected but actually conferred status and
prestige. It also provided an extension, both
physically and psychologically, of the home – and
British domestic building (it can scarcely be
called 'architecture') was second to none in its
space-wasting, uncomfortable pretentiousness.
No wonder the cars were like that too.

Below
1922 Austin Seven

At last, in 1948, came a Motor Show. The smug and the stuffy were still in evidence, but now there were wonderful new cars to enchant and seduce the public. The American industry exhibited grandly scaled and imaginatively styled whoppers that were better than anything else in the world for American circumstances, but woefully inappropriate to Britain or Europe – it hardly mattered though, for nobody was allowed to import them and they were there purely for show. The French, makers of beautiful *voitures de grand tourisme* such as Delage, Delahaye and Lago Talbot, also charmed visitors with some delightful miniatures: the 4CV Renault so modern in its detail, or the 2CV Citroën so rigorously logical in its minimalism. Fiat, most sympathetic and supportive of the idea of cars for the people, did not yet consider themselves ready to exhibit. Volkswagen, whose efficient Beetle's origins in the Nazi Kraft durch Freude movement brought the expression 'People's Car' into some disrepute, were in a similar pickle.

Above The brilliant 2CV Citroën in 1948

Above, top The 1948 London Motor Show. Hudson, Delahaye, Studebaker, Morris, Panhard… How the picture has faded!

Above An early design
for a Morris Minor
advertisement

Yet, while Anglophile visitors to the Show were
overwhelmed by the ravishing new Jaguar XK120,
the spiteful-looking Frazer-Nash, or the vast and
highly individual Allard, the star exhibit at a more
modest and accessible level was a wonderfully
promising Morris Minor, successor to the old
Morris Eight. A little over twelve feet long and
five feet wide, its shape echoed the bulbous
contours of the bigger new Morris models, its
engine was the feeble old faithful side-valver, its
front suspension was right up to date, and its
designer was Mr Alec Issigonis.

Less than four years later, the Nuffield Group (which owned Morris, among other things) merged with Austin. The Minor acquired an Austin engine, and a man named Leonard Lord acquired a sense of satisfaction. Lord came from nowhere, via a scholarship to a Coventry public school, to the drawing offices successively of Courtaulds, Daimler and Hotchkiss. When William Morris bought Hotchkiss (who used to make the engines for the famous old 'Bullnose' Morris car) he recognised Lord's worth and gave him executive powers that were used with what might politely be called vigour. Eventually the two men fell out, and Lord went off to work for Austin, vowing that he would get Morris in the end. By 1950 he was in a position to propose a merger with his old firm; in 1952 it happened, with the creation of the British Motor Corporation, the first of nine administrative entities responsible for the Mini in its long career.

When the merger came, Issigonis went, fearing that political squabbles would interfere with his work there. He went to Alvis, then making handsome but ineffectual classic cars and ugly but excellent military vehicles, not to mention some air-cooled radial aero-engines. For two or three years he was hard at work on an all-new high-performance car, which he designed completely from stem to stern, engine and all. He was, as we were saying, a good engineer.

That model was by all accounts a very good car, but Alvis decided against making it and scrapped the prototype, feeling that they would fare better and spend less producing a new aero-engine for the increasingly popular helicopter trade. For Issigonis it was all good experience, especially in his work on the car's all-independent rubber-sprung suspension; but he was left feeling a little lost until, late in 1955, Sir Leonard Lord, as he was now known, telephoned to ask him to come back. Early in 1956, Issigonis did so, and gladly, for he appreciated Lord: 'A tough, wonderful man with a fantastic personality, a born businessman and a great production engineer.'

Top Leonard Lord
Above Lord Nuffield

Left *In hoc signo vinces*... Newly formed BMC awarded themselves a rosette

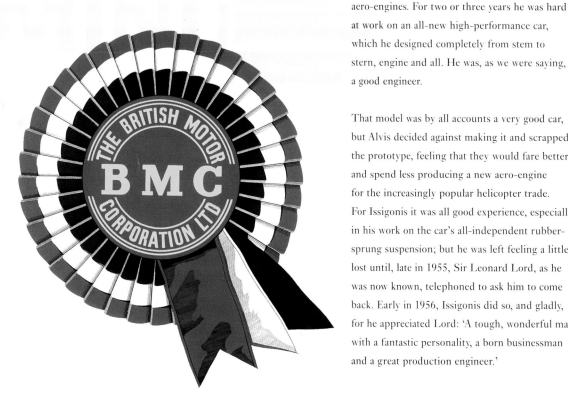

In that same year the Suez Crisis, which had inflamed the Middle East in 1954, flared up again, this time very seriously. Egypt closed the Canal; Arab confederates in Syria cut the oil pipeline crossing that country; and the military war that had been nipped in the bud by violent conflicts of diplomatic interest was replaced by an economic war, at the heart of which was a sudden and severe shortage of petrol throughout Europe. As a result, Britain resumed rationing, with private motorists allowed only ten gallons a month. There was no foreseeable prospect of the situation becoming any easier.

In Germany and Italy, where life was as yet more austere than in Britain and fuel economy therefore already important, there had been developments in car design to achieve real economies. Iso in Italy had been the first to create a 'bubble car', perhaps the nearest thing to a protoplasmal primordial atomic globule that the

motoring world had yet seen. This Isetta – later taken up by BMW – had a 236cc two-stroke engine in its sharply tapering tail, with a full-width side-hinged door at the front and barely 7.5 feet between the extremities. An even earlier design, featuring tandem seating and a side-hinged aircraft-style canopy, was put into production by Messerschmitt in Germany. Two years later, another erstwhile aircraft manufacturer, Heinkel, presented a cleverly structured bubble car with an engine of only 175cc and again a full-width side-hinged front door.

Left The Lightweight Special

There were others, British and foreign and considerably more reprehensible; but the best of these smooth-contoured bubble cars were very clever pieces of work. An aircraft manufacturer could be relied on to be ingenious and exact in structure and materials. Anything so light was bound to be economical and not necessarily lacking in liveliness. Anything so extraordinarily compact was likewise bound to be a revelation in ease of parking and agility in city traffic. There were thousands in Britain and Europe who applauded the originality and purposefulness of these novel designs; who approved of the emancipation they promised; and who were happy to accept the compromises these basic cars demanded in exchange for the low costs of short-range motoring that they guaranteed.

There were many others who ridiculed or even hated these microbes. The bubble cars did not look anything like what the unimaginative thought cars should look like. They did not demand the same driving disciplines as ordinary cars. They would have an unfair advantage in being able to park nose in to the kerb, so that the occupants could open the front door and step straight on to the pavement. Worse still, and indeed the most serious objection often advanced against rear-engined small cars from mainland Europe, was that, in the absence of a 'proper' bonnet (preferably with a hefty engine within it), the occupants' feet would be too close to the accident that was always assumed to be head on.

Sir Leonard Lord was one of the people who hated them. 'God damn these bloody awful bubble cars,' he said to Issigonis. 'We must drive them out of the streets by designing a proper miniature car.' It was the same philosophy as had impelled Herbert Austin to challenge the crude and often dangerous cycle cars of the boom times after the Great War (not to mention the motorcycle-and-sidecar combinations that were all many a working family man could afford) with the baby Austin Seven. And it was the start of the Mini.

The idea appealed to Issigonis. He was most at ease with small things, which he saw as presenting an intellectual challenge absent in the creation of big things. The big cars of his time bored him. Even his Alvis prototype had been more compact than its prospective rivals. He had, as he said, been weaned on Austin Sevens. With help from his friend George Dowson, before the war he had built an exquisite little racing single-seater called the Lightweight Special, a hand-made marvel of minimalism. In *Wind, Sand and Stars*, the airman and novelist Antoine de Saint-Exupéry wrote, 'In anything at all, perfection is finally attained not when there is no longer anything to add, but when there is no longer anything to be taken away.' That was how Issigonis felt.

It was in March 1957, while the diplomats of six mainland European nations were in Rome setting up the European Common Market, that in the Kremlin (the denizens' nickname for the Austin headquarters at Longbridge, Birmingham) other projects were put aside and work concentrated on what was to be the Mini. It was a small team, only eight men, who worked with Issigonis, translating the freehand sketches in which he expressed his concepts most clearly and concisely.

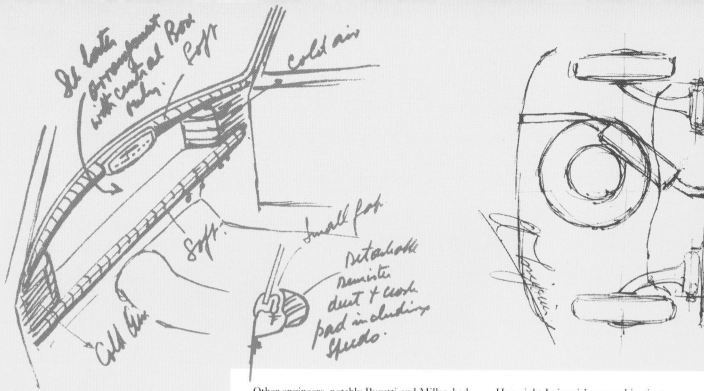

It is questionable whether Issigonis could have been a fine artist, as was his opposite number at Fiat, the similarly long-fingered and sensitive Dante Giacosa, whose relaxation was botanical drawing. It is improbable that he could have been a great painter like Leonardo da Vinci; but, if you look at the technical sketches of Leonardo when he was studying anatomy or fluid flow or working as a military engineering consultant, you will see a severe practicality in them, a no-nonsense resort to pencil and paper as a language for the discussion of form and content and process, that is strikingly like the sketches of Issigonis. The men around him knew him, could understand what he was saying in pictures, could translate his expressions into engineering drawings or directly into metal as the occasion demanded. He was thus freed to let his ideas flow, be it in large-scale perspectives or in thumbnail doodles.

Other engineers, notably Bugatti and Miller, had in their times displayed a gift for appreciating the distribution of stresses in a solid metal component. Issigonis applied a similar talent to boxlike fabrications of metal sheet. Once his sketches had been transmuted into metal, he began to work as a sculptor works, moving masses into different positions until his trained eye and conditioned instinct told him that they were right.

The story of his final proportioning of the Morris Minor is famous, but like all great stories it will bear repetition. The car had been completed as a mock-up, but Issigonis felt uncomfortable about it, thought something was wrong, thought it might look better wider. He had his men cut it straight down the middle and move the two halves apart until it looked right, whereupon the insertion of a four-inch gusset was the final step. The mock-up design then went on to the detailers in preparation for production. Later he was to do exactly the same – except that the width of the insert was only two inches – to his prototype Mini.

How right Issigonis's eye and instinct were was quickly confirmed when the Minor came on the market, for it was an immediate success and remained a success for so long that it eventually caused its makers some embarrassment: whenever they sought to terminate its career to make way for new models, an enraptured public would not allow it. The little car had been judged to such a nicety that its balance, its roadholding and its handling had become legendary.

Part of the secret lay in the suspension of the car, this being something in which Issigonis had long taken a particular interest. He was by no means one of those designers who could work only in the off-hand manner already described, as though conducting a small orchestra of metal-shapers: his earlier years in the industry had required him to earn his keep – and his employers' respect – as a design draughtsman. He never went to the extreme of being a designer obsessed with academic theory, though the extent of his formal qualifications being limited to a diploma in mechanical engineering. Like many another great creator who knows what is right and is quite content to let some menial calculator confirm it afterwards, he loathed mathematics. 'All creative people hate mathematics,' he insisted. 'It's the most uncreative subject you can study, unless you become an Einstein and study it in the abstract philosophical sense.'

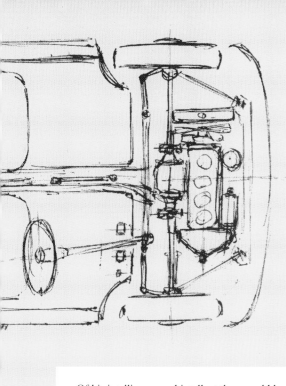

Of his intelligence and intellect there could be no doubt whatever. Issigonis was an extremely cultivated man, wide-ranging in his conversation, perceptive in his judgements, gently mocking in his wit, devoted and sincere in his personal relationships. Such a gentle man was even a little out of place in the motor industry, a scene which, especially in Britain, was hardly one to attract either a first-class brain or a fastidious temperament. The truth was that, after all hope of a broader education had been dispelled by his family's enforced flight from Smyrna (now Izmir) in 1922, it seemed to his marine engineer father that training in engineering would give the then seventeen-year-old Alexander Arnold Constantine Issigonis a good start. After passing his examinations, his first job was in a London design office where he worked on a semi-automatic transmission for cars. This was doomed to fail because General Motors brought out synchromesh at just about that time, and amid a worldwide slump it was a much cheaper and therefore more attractive proposition than the necessarily more complex automatic.

So Issigonis accepted an offer to work for Humber in Coventry, where he came under William Heynes (later to be chief designer at Jaguar) and began to specialize in suspension. He made a lot of progress, helping to develop new forms of independent suspension for the Humber and Hillman models of 1936. Then he moved again, this time to the Morris factory near Oxford. Once more he specialized in suspension, studying and learning to admire the work of Maurice Olley, that expatriate Englishman who had gone from Rolls-Royce to General Motors and there revolutionized chassis and suspension design through the first theoretical examination of the science of steering, roadholding and handling.

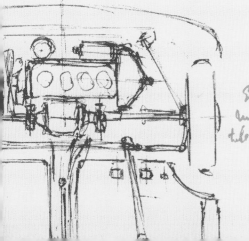

Left However did *you* get one?

By that time Issigonis was engaged in the construction of the Lightweight Special mentioned earlier. Built with hand tools on a shoestring, this car had some claim to being the most advanced competition machine of its time, and one of the most passionate machines of all time. It really was a lightweight, totalling only 587 pounds, of which the highly tuned Austin Seven engine accounted for no less than 38%. It was not merely the work of mechanics: it was a work of art, and a means of acquiring science. There was scarcely an ounce wasted in it anywhere, nor any significant space. When, twenty years afterwards, Issigonis was creating the Mini, all his knowledge of structures, his experience with suspension, his concern for minutiae, and his originality of ideas, combined in support of the art that he had developed with the Minor – the art of putting things in the right place.

That really was the secret of the Mini. There had been other cars with front-wheel drive, some of them even with transverse engines, going back in history to the first decade of the century. There had been others with rubber suspension, or with the admirable stability born of having a wheel at each corner, or with bodies aggressively boxy in shape so as to secure the maximum habitable space within limiting dimensions. There had also been many others employing the BMC A-type engine that Issigonis was constrained to employ when the firm's chairman, Sir Leonard Lord, asked him to produce his technically advanced bestseller. What Issigonis did was to arrange the necessary components in a way that had not been done before, subjugating the machinery that had traditionally occupied the lion's share of the motor-car to the requirements of the people who would buy and occupy it. It was an essentially humanistic concept: he was not designing a car for engineers, nor for motoring enthusiasts, but quite simply for people, a car in which 80% was theirs to occupy as they liked.

There were really only four elements that were crucial to his design, four things upon which his speculative ideas depended: front-wheel drive, a gearbox sharing the same casing as the engine, the Birfield joint, and the ten-inch tyre. Given these, everything he envisaged could be brought about.

Issigonis had been convinced of the appropriateness of front wheel drive as the result of an experimental front-drive Minor that he confected in a spirit of curiosity before he left for Alvis. A small space-efficient car had to dispense with a drive shaft connecting the engine and the final drive, so either the engine had to go in the tail and drive the rear wheels – an undoubtedly cheap method favoured by Fiat and VW – or it must sit in the nose and drive the front wheels, a method favoured by Citroën and known to impart better directional stability, but made complex and costly by the need of the front wheels not only to bump up and down but also to steer. Other front-drive cars were burdened by huge hubs to accommodate complex universal joints at the outer extremes of the shafts that drove the wheels, but in the Mini such grossness would be untenable. The solution was found in a design dating back to 1926 by a Czech engineer, Hans Rzeppa. By 1957 it was known as the Birfield joint, and was being made in England by Hardy Spicer for use in some naturally obscure, and doubtless secret, control gear in submarines. With it the Mini could be both driven and steered without the sudden seizures and vibrations that would be felt without it. Front-wheel drive, which put more weight over the front wheels to the benefit of traction in very small cars, was therefore admissible.

Right Crucial component: the Birfield-Rzeppa cv joint

WIZARDRY
ON WHEELS

THE REVOLUTIONARY

"QUALITY FIRST"

MORRIS

850

If the engine were not to waste inordinate space, it must be installed transversely. Everybody knew that an engine was always aligned fore-and-aft – everybody except Walter Christie, an American who between 1905 and 1907 made some frightening seventeen-litre racers and later made valuable contributions to the design of the Russian T34 tank; and Dante Giacosa, whose brilliant 600cc prototype Fiat of 1947 was squashed by the management. Issigonis, who enjoyed the confidence of Sir Leonard Lord, would not tolerate anybody else interfering, and had his way, installing the engine transversely.

In which case, where was the gearbox to go? He had briefly toyed with a two-cylinder engine cut out of the regular four-cylinder A-series engine, but its promise of economy was nothing like so huge as its threat of vibrational fatigue. Although it had made room for a gearbox on the end, it had to be forgotten. Resuming his pencilled cogitations, Issigonis came up with the idea of putting the gearbox underneath the engine. The clutch, which was a consumable item in those days, could be left accessible on the end of the crankshaft, but the shafts carrying the assorted cogs would lie directly beneath it, and that would mean engine and gears sharing the same lubricating oil – a prospect about which there was some justifiable worry. Even if it was proved by the oil people to be a bad practice, it was overall a good solution.

Above A 4-seated box with the machinery brushed across the front. This ghosted image of a brilliant design is accurate and honest enough to display the offset angle of the steering wheel

Having solved this enigma, Issigonis could now settle down to the layout of his passenger compartment, the big box that followed the little one (containing the engine) down the road. He aimed to get four people (and some baggage) into a box 8.5 feet long, and, now that he could pack all the machinery into a mere 18 inches, he could achieve his aim of a car only 10 feet long. There remained the bulky wheelarches as unwelcome intrusions. How to minimize them?

Far better than they were thirty, or even fifteen years earlier, the tyres of those days were nevertheless pretty awful, imposing severe limits on car performance and design. Although they were skinny, they were prey to centrifugal force, expanding in diameter as the speed rose, and in danger of rupture if it rose too far. Keeping rotational speed down meant having a large diameter, so even small cars had wheels at least twelve or as much fourteen inches in diameter, usually carrying tyres less than five inches wide on their narrow rims. In the prospective Mini, there could not be room for such monstrosities, and in any case their weight, because it was unsprung, would be adverse to good suspension behaviour. Praying that Dunlop, major contractors for tyres and wheels, would be able to make the idea work, Issigonis shocked them with a proposition for wheels only eight inches across, happily settling as a compromise on the size that he actually wanted, which was ten inches. With a tyre a little wider than five inches, for the sake not only of comfort and grip but also of keeping heat build-up at bay, the spatial needs of the Mini could be met.

Rubber was used for space saving in another way. Calling on his experience with rubber suspension in the Lightweight Special and in the Alvis prototype, he summoned the aid of another of those rare men of brain and sensitivity, Dr Alex Moulton. The son of a man famous in the rubber industry, he had worked with Issigonis on the Alvis, and now helped scheme a set of rubber springs for the Mini. Many of the characteristics of rubber as an engineering material could be deemed prejudicial to this task, but the two men took the view that those same characteristics could be helpful if cleverly exploited. And so, on balance, it proved.

All this work was done at a furious rate. A wooden mock-up of the body, and others of the main mechanical items, could be inspected by Sir Leonard in July 1957, only four months after he gave Issigonis the go-ahead. That was a momentous month. On Saturday 20 July, at Aintree, CAS (Tony) Brooks and Stirling Moss shared the driving of the Vanwall which won the British Grand Prix, the first time that the event had been won by an all-British combination of car and drivers. That same day, sixty miles away in Bradford, the Prime Minister, Mr Harold Macmillan, was telling a cheering Conservative Party Conference, 'Let's be frank about it: most of our people have never had it so good.'

Below Was ever a door more sensibly contrived?

Left The photographer's angle disguises the steering-wheel offset

It was going to get better. In October there were two running Mini prototypes, painted bright orange, out on the road. Most of their development mileage was done on a disused aerodrome at Chalgrove, during which they prompted only three major modifications.

One was to turn the entire engine assembly through 180 degrees, so that the carburettors (and the exhaust pipes) faced rearward: carburettor icing problems had been troublesome when they had faced forward, just behind the car's frontal grille. There was one beneficial effect: the engine-driven fan could now blow cooling air through the side-mounted 'radiator' heat exchanger more efficiently than it had previously sucked it through. The detrimental aspect, not noted at the time, was that hot air blown into the left-front wheelarch prompted overheating and premature deterioration, if not occasional failure, of the left-front tyre. The rearrangement also required another gear in the sump, otherwise the car would have had four reverse gears and one forward; but the revised gears cost another 4% in power losses.

There was to be more power lost. The prototype, with a 948cc engine as first seen in the Austin A30 in 1951, was found to be capable of easily exceeding ninety mph. At a time when most small cars could barely manage seventy, and some had to struggle to top sixty, this seemed a bit too much: it was inconsistent with the concept, and it was probably asking too much of the brakes and those new little tyres. With no great sense of disappointment, the engine capacity was reduced to 848cc.

The third change was seen to be necessary during protracted endurance running round the bumpy Chalgrove perimeter track. Metal fatigue was developing around the points where the suspension was attached to the body, something potentially disastrous in a unitary or stressed-skin structure. The answer was to interpose sub-frames, one at the rear carrying the suspension there, another at the front carrying not only the suspension but also the entire engine-transmission assembly. These sub-frames may have been cursed as rust havens in later years, but at the time they did a wonderful job not only in distributing loads into the hull in a less stressful way, but also in insulating the passenger box from the engine and road noises that had previously enjoyed all too direct a path to the inmates' ears.

Above One of the prototypes…

Above ...before the engine was reversed

There were numerous other problems cropping up – there always are – but nothing seemed terribly serious or insurmountable. Other people, after all, were having at least as much trouble, though Issigonis did not, or was supposed not to, know. Lord had privily hedged his bets by setting ERA, the erstwhile makers of racing cars, to come up with an alternative design. The principals in this enterprise were David Hodkin, then considered a very bright young man recently come down from Cambridge, and Laurence Pomeroy. The latter was the son of the engineer who created the 20hp Vauxhall which trounced the Rolls-Royce in the RAC Reliability Trials of 1908. In the 1950s, Laurence Pomeroy was well established as the technical editor of *The Motor* and a constant agitator for advanced engineering. The design that ERA promoted featured an air-cooled aluminium engine set transversely across the tail of the car, with pneumatic suspension and huge and well-meant but ill-sited tail fins. Tooling up for this little *jeu d'esprit* would have been impossibly costly; when in July 1958 Issigonis took Lord for a ride around Longbridge in the prototype Mini, Lord was convinced, demanding that it be in production in twelve months. 'I shall sign the cheques,' he said encouragingly. 'You get on with getting the thing to work.'

Right Laika
Below Hovercraft
prototype by Saunders
Roe, 1959

To set up production in a year might seem a daunting task in an industry where much work was still done by old-fashioned methods. This was, however, an age in which technological advances were coming thick and fast, advances compared with which the most dazzling achievements of the motor industry might be seen as trivial. In that very same 1958, some momentous developments were taking place. The De Havilland Comet began the first regular jet airline service across the Atlantic, to be followed soon by the Boeing 707. An entirely new kind of vehicle, the Hovercraft, was invented by a Suffolk boatbuilder named Christopher Cockerell. The US Navy's prodigious nuclear-powered submarine Nautilus was revealed as having travelled submerged from Pearl Harbour, under the Arctic icecap and via the North Pole, to Iceland. Marvellous nuclear-power stations were beginning to proliferate in Britain, France and the USA. Out in space, a dog named Laika was orbiting Earth in the Soviet Union's second satellite, to be kept remote company when the USA at last succeeded in putting a grapefruit-sized satellite, Explorer 2, in space. Maintaining their lead, in 1959 the Russians launched Lunik 2, the first Moon-landing rocket.

The motoring world was not without its achievements as well. When Mike Hawthorn won the world championship of drivers, it was at the end of a season in which for the first time (at the instigation of the oil companies, who were putting a great deal of money into the sport) Grand Prix cars were restricted to 'pump' petrol. In Italy, Pirelli began marketing their fabric-belted radial ply tyre, the Cinturato, addressing the shortcomings (and avoiding the patents) of the pioneering Michelin X. In Holland, DAF produced a small car featuring a brilliant steplessly variable transmission. In the USA, Ford produced the Edsel, as sad a mistake as marketing experts ever made, and one such as Issigonis never made.

In Britain, developments to ease motoring were slow. Twenty-three years after Germany, and 34 years after Italy, Britain opened its first main road with motorway regulations, a petty little bypass round Preston in Lancashire. It seemed shameful to those who recalled that a scheme to link London and Liverpool by motorway had been carried as far as a Private Member's Bill in Parliament before being dropped – in 1924! The first motorway, the M1, connecting London to Birmingham would be opened in 1959. Britain could, however still be obstructive to the car: it was in 1958 that the London police began to use radar for catching those who broke the speed limit, and that London introduced parking meters. Yet, everywhere in the developed world, it was upon the motor car that personal ambitions were focused.

Above right The M1
motorway, clean and new
Right Time is money

Issigonis saw his Mini as the car that would liberate the confined, emancipate the undertrodden. But, when it came, it did not work like that: it was not working-class families who flocked to buy this amazingly sympathetic and impressively affordable car. Nor, at first, did anybody else. It would take time and good propaganda (by this time people called it 'public relations') to educate and encourage customers hesitating either from doubt or from sheer bewilderment.

How luxurious can an Austin Seven get?

AUS 61

Most people are very nicely satisfied thank you with *any* Austin Seven. Others want the earth. The new Austin Super Seven has been designed for them. It's got everything any other Austin Seven's got—high m.p.h. (70), high m.p.g. (50), large space inside (for seating four adults), small-space outside (for parking in 11 feet). *And it's got much more. Here's what.*

INSIDE New duotone trim in subtly blending colour-choices. Sound insulation to hush the engine to a gentle purr. Fuller cushions for greater comfort: thick new carpets. New oval-shaped instrument panel, including both oil-pressure and water-temperature gauges. And many many more extras.

OUT New duotone palette of brilliant colours to choose from. Much more dashing fine-mesh grille. It's altogether a gayer, brighter car. Add up the list of improvements when you see the new model at your Austin dealer. Price: £405 plus £186.17.3 Purchase Tax and surcharge

GET INTO AN AUSTIN AND OUT OF THE ORDINARY

NEW AUSTIN SUPER SEVEN

THE AUSTIN MOTOR COMPANY LIMITED · LONGBRIDGE · BIRMINGHAM

By Appointment to
Her Majesty The Queen
Motor Car Manufacturers
The Austin Motor
Company Limited

Backed by BMC 12-month
warranty and BMC service

The new AUSTIN SE7EN

Mini
Upstart

Below If they could pack all that stuff into the car, these people were truly the incredible seven

The car was officially launched on 26 August 1959. Issigonis and his team had met Lord's target and several thousand Minis had been built and delivered to dealers far and wide. Pictures had already been seen in the press, and there was a storm of publicity when the official day came. Motoring journalists and motoring writers had been brought, just a week earlier, to the FVRDE – the Fighting Vehicles Research and Development Establishment – run under the aegis of the Ministry of Defence and under a moderately opaque cloak of security at Chobham in Surrey. The Mini was not expected to go galumphing over the rough tracks meant for tanks and scout cars, but there was a banked, high-speed oval track; a sinuous road twisting through the trees up and down a steep hill; a large, level steering pad (or skid pad, if you provoked your vehicle to its limits); and some accurately elevated gradients. It was a very useful car-testing facility, where the Mini could be put through its paces.

Several of the visiting journalists found the new car so different from anything in their experience that they were baffled and did not know what to judge it against. A large proportion of the motoring press in those days was very slow to criticize, conscious that they ultimately owed their jobs to the manufacturers who would buy advertizing space in their papers. A noble exception was *Motor Sport* under its staunchly independent editor William Boddy. Before long there would be another, to be known for a few months as *Small Car and Mini Owner* and eventually as *Car*, given its unrelentingly honest character by a young and soon notorious editor, Doug Blain.

You would have had to hunt, over the next few months, for any substantial criticism of the flaws the original Mini did reveal. The ventilation, for example, was a problem. The doors carried sliding windows so as to liberate the utmost elbow room and give the occupants a feeling of more space in the interior, and the plan was that when these opened for ventilation the rear quarter windows should also be hinged open, so that air drawn in at the front could be vented out at the rear, where a low-pressure region created by the speed of the car would draw it out. It was an excellent theory that worked beautifully in some earlier cars from other manufacturers, but in the Mini it failed on two counts. One was that the supposed low-pressure zone was often in fact a high-pressure one – because the bluff body shape provoked unpredictable airflow – so the rear windows would be slammed shut again. The other was that in the basic Mini, the much-vaunted version costing just under £500, the rear windows were fixed.

There were problems with misting of the windows, too, for it was not until 1961 that a fresh-air heater was offered. Earlier heaters, after the fashion of the day among cheaper cars, merely recirculated the cabin air, humidity notwithstanding. Theoretically it was possible to buy a basic Mini without a heater; in practice, it was almost impossible, for the extra item of equipment helped the Corporation to find a bit more profit where the rock-bottom pricing of the car left very little.

Right Windows sliding fore and aft are better than those which rise and fall

The price came as a great surprise when it was announced. It looked as though the BMC were intending to challenge the crude and primitive Ford Popular, later to be known as the Ford 8, the only thing on the market that was significantly cheaper, when all other conceivable rivals to the Mini cost far more. In retrospect the price was a mistake, brought about perhaps by the marketing department sharing the Issigonis idea of a car for the less well-off.

Nobody thought of the price when they found the floor awash. A lapped joint between two of the sheet-steel pressings forming the undersurface of the car had been designed (redesigned, actually – it happened when they were turning the engine round) so that it faced the wrong way, scooping up water carried in the turbulent air passing between the car and a wet road. It took three months to find the cause of that problem. Meanwhile, each body had its hollows filled with a plastics foam which, growing rigid as it cooled, actually made a substantial improvement in the body's already excellent torsional stiffness.

Stiffness in the wrong place occasioned another regular complaint. Exhausts used to fracture because they lacked the flexibility to accommodate the movement of the engine on its normal flexible bearers.

These and other faults all received urgent attention, and eventually were suitably fixed. Sometimes it was easy: the ignition distributor, immediately behind the grille now that the engine had been switched through 180 degrees, was often soused on wet days, but sleeving or shielding it was a simple task. One of the most fundamental

faults, however, never received much attention, mainly because not many people noticed it and nothing could be done about it. The engine, with no less than eighteen assorted transmission gears occupying its sump, treated its oil very cruelly. Because none of these gears was of worm or hypoid type, the designers gambled on regular engine oil (SAE 30 normally, or 20 in really cold conditions) being able to lubricate the gearbox, final drive and differential gears all tucked away down below the crankshaft. Fresh new engine oil could, for a while; but, like most forecourt oils even today, it contained a number of vital additives, one of the most important being a peculiar sort of microscopic plastics spaghetti known as a 'viscosity index improver'. Its job was to prevent the oil becoming too thin as it grew hot, but it could not survive being caught between meshing gears (a predicament for which it was never intended) and they would chop it up until it was more like mostaccioli than spaghetti. The result was that, after a couple of thousand miles, the oil in the sump of a Mini had lost a lot of its ability to protect the engine, and not everybody was punctilious about changing the oil as frequently as they should.

Nor did they wax keen in attending to the needs of chassis lubrication, which involved the application of a grease gun to twelve points every thousand miles. Ten years earlier that would have been thought normal; ten years later it would be thought insufferable. The Mini was born on the cusp of a new era – and in more ways than one.

Without real precedent, the Mini is sometimes seen in retrospect as the cause of the social changes that began to be evident around 1960. The little car might decently claim some part in the encouragement of the new scheme of things, but honestly nothing more. In truth it was simply a product of the pressures that brought about the social changes. It was just remarkable that the new era seemed to begin so soon after the Mini had come on to the stage.

The speed and completeness of the change was due to the one element that had been missing from earlier social revolutions: modern communications. With radio and, even more importantly, television now prevailing everywhere over the old-fashioned newspaper (which was doomed to become an instrument of comment and entertainment), people could be told and shown the news with unprecedented immediacy; could be harangued and swayed by clever manipulation of fact and opinion in rapid response to any new circumstance of politics or economics, real or fabricated.

So when people everywhere were offered what appeared to be a new deal – it was offered specifically to the young and maturing – they swallowed the idea whole. In the aftermath of the Second World War, people had been resentful of the social structure that they believed had been responsible for it. They resolved to teach their children how wrong it was, and they did what they could to topple it. In Britain particularly there arose an optimistic vision of an undifferentiated society in which the progressive levelling out of incomes would become a permanent feature, while the instal-lation of a universal middle class would almost totally eliminate the really rich and the really poor. All this was to be achieved through semi-spontaneous, semi-planned social evolution, which would combine with the increasing national affluence to steer the country towards the classless society.

It turned out to be a fake deal, off the bottom of the pack, but these ideals were immensely influential while they lasted. The particular effect that they had on the British motoring scene was deepened by the availability of the Mini as a new expression of what classlessness meant.

But it was not, as Issigonis had expected, the working classes who first flocked to the Mini. A car technically so unusual would be too risky an undertaking for a man who could not take risks with his money. Nor were the rich yet ready to stoop to something calling itself the Austin Seven or, even more apologetically, the Morris Mini-Minor – names that had been chosen by the marketing people to comfort prospective buyers with fond thoughts of past times. Those who tackled it first were, as so often, the middle classes, the folk who had a bit of money and a bit of education and a bit of a reputation for supplying men of thought and men of action when they were needed.

The Mini cost £500. Never mind what other cars might cost – how much capital could people call upon? When the Mini appeared, the figures had not changed much since a survey nine years earlier, when 62.4% of the population over the age of 25 had less than £100 at their disposal. The next largest percentage, 26.8%, had something between £100 and £1000; and the next 9.2% could turn to anything up to £10,000. Ignoring the very rich, the two last-mentioned groups of people numbered more than 11 million, and mustered more than 43% of the nation's private wealth.

AUSTIN Incredible **mini** Saloon . . . .

★ Combined ignition/starter switch.
★ Safety sun visors and interior mirror.
★ Two-leading-shoe brakes at front.
★ Greater torque capacity gearbox.

. . now with Hydrolastic suspension!

IT'S WIZARDRY ON WHEELS!

The Revolutionary
"QUALITY FIRST"
MORRIS *Mini-Minor*

Left Production – linear motion

That was more than enough people to constitute a Mini market, and it needed only enough time for the virtues of the car to filter through into the minds of the public and allay the doubts still lurking there. For the first year, sales were slow, and so were the Minis. Too many Minis were to be seen and heard crawling around suburban streets, as likely as not with their poor little engines slogging painfully at the lowest possible speed in top gear (which was actually about 14mph), faltering at corners and junctions because Everybody Knew that small cars were underpowered and unstable and it was dangerous to be enterprising in them. Luckily, it only took the enterprises of a few mature drivers in the expert class and a few more young drivers in the audacious class to broadcast the message far and fast that the Mini was enormous fun when driven briskly.

The mature types were the road-testers of the motoring press who, whatever their views on the structure, layout and detail of the Mini, were unanimous in finding its acceleration unexpectedly lively for its class and its roadholding and handling exceptional regardless of class. Carrying its weight low, and with track and wheelbase as great as possible in relation to the overall dimensions, the car was naturally disposed to fast cornering and quick steering. It was given a pressure-limiting valve to prevent the rear brakes from locking prematurely in a crash stop. It was given, quite early in the development stages, by the ex-Wolseley chief development engineer Charles Griffin, pronounced toe-in of the rear wheels to prevent understeer growing excessive. It needed faith in its abilities. As experience grew, faith did likewise.

Its career in sporting competition would soon confirm its abilities, but as the young generation cottoned on to the Mini they began to demonstrate its agility. This did not always please the onlookers: a lot of hostility to the car was generated by the incredibly bad manners (or, seen in another light, the incredible enjoyment) of some drivers, who used the proficiency of the car to perform antics that looked a lot more dangerous than they truly were. Exhibitionist presentation of the Mini, festooned as it soon could be with gaudy trinkets and trimmings, also offended some people. But, the more the staid and proper objected, the more the impertinent and the impenitent revelled in the improprieties that the Mini made possible. To drive a Mini was to cock a snook.

There is, according to the experts, no such thing as bad publicity. The cult of the Mini grew rapidly; but that cult was not entirely welcomed even by its creators. Issigonis lamented that, having endowed the Mini with an extra 70%

Above 1964 Morris Mini Cooper S

cornering power (compared with the average small car) as a safety margin, he was dismayed to find that, as soon as they discovered this margin, Mini drivers used it up. If they then had an accident, it might be 70% more violent. More often than not though, the Minis of the first few years were bought and used as the modest and economical little cars that they were intended to be.

The Mini was enabled to grow strong (the tales of the Cooper and Cooper S, among other giant-killers, are told in a later chapter) or to grow long (the tale of the vans is also to be told), but it was not allowed to grow up. To this day – whatever may be the differences in engines, in wheels and tyres, in fixtures and fittings, in its provision for safety and conservation and ecology and compliance with innumerable regulations – the Mini is essentially what it has always been. That is the secret of its longevity.

They changed the name of the Austin Seven to Austin Mini. Then they changed its sibling to Morris Mini, without any Minority. Eventually both brand names were dropped and the Mini was just that. BMC became successively British Leyland, Leyland Cars, BL, BL Cars, Austin Morris, Austin Rover, and Rover Group, while the effective proprietors have ranged from Leyland Motors through the British Government to British Aerospace and most recently BMW, whose leader Bernd Pischetsrieder (1993-99) was not only a fan of the Mini but also a relation of Issigonis.

They changed the suspension of the car, for a few years. Dr Moulton was very keen on hydraulic intermodulation of suspension units, after the admirable fashion of Citroën but employing cheaper components and materials (rubber and water, in particular) and investigating various ways of interconnecting the car's corners. It was a mistake: it did, as intended, mollify the rubber-sprung Mini's slightly bumpy ride, but, because the car's wheelbase was so much shorter than that of the French car, the change was wrought at the expense of a pitching tendency that was much more disturbing.

They changed the shape of the Mini nose for a few years, too. Customers were told that it was a styling improvement that also liberated more space under the bonnet. It was suspected that it was a change to accommodate newly rigorous requirements in headlamp positioning and impact absorption. Everyone was generally rather relieved when it reverted to the original snubby little nose that was so much a part of the car's pert character.

Below A Morris Mini Minor, 1959

Above One of the first Austin Minis, 1959

Right Less, said the architect Mies van der Rohe, is more

The Mini had seen a glassfibre-reinforced plastics body in South America, where Chilean legislation demanded (as did the Swiss) locally made bodies if foreign cars were to be assembled there. The external seams, beloved of Mini enthusiasts and originally a means of cheapening and simplifying the production tooling, vanished. They disappeared from a few other Minis as well, along with the external door hinges, which had been designed to allow for low-grade labour on foreign assembly lines.

Quite a few items, from steering wheels to engines, were adopted from the Metro when that well-meant and quite obliging little car came to market. The Mini is still in production; the Metro is not. They even gave the Mini a splendidly clever automatic transmission, one of the few subsequent losses that should be deeply lamented.

The customers made their own changes. As time passed, different people stepped into the showrooms. There came a time when the working man or woman looking for fairly basic transport was the usual customer, just as Issigonis had expected. There came a time when the reason for buying a Mini was a fondness for times past when a Mini was a fashion statement or a declaration of lifestyle. There came a time when a Mini was bought just for fun.

The manufacturers were alive to these changing demands on the Mini. They gave it at various times an electric fan for the 'radiator', bumper overriders, adjustable seats, different instruments, wind-down windows (a terrible shame), and an incredible assortment of superficialities calculated to make it more dignified, more cheeky, more dowdy, more chic, more distinguished or more vulgar. They gave sometimes with one hand while taking away with the other. They made changes, sometimes of necessity and sometimes speculatively, time and time again, sometimes year by year. *Plus ça change, plus c'est la même chose.*

I'm very proud that it has run for so long...

Sir Alec Issigonis

'One of the most responsive, sensible and just plain wonderful fun cars ever made.'

PAUL SKILLETER journalist

fashion
statement
irreverent
Gamine
endearing

Was it really Mary Quant who, as is popularly supposed, created the miniskirt? Academics – and it may be a fine sign of progress that they can concern themselves with such things – are not convinced that it was she. If not, then who?

Might it not have been Issigonis himself? Consider the nature of his Mini. It was no bigger than absolutely necessary. It did all that was really required. It was cheap to make and to buy. It gave people a mobility, an ease of manoeuvre, beyond their previous experience. It looked unlike anything that had gone before, but it looked convincing, pert, and (once we had grown accustomed to its initially shocking abnormality) positively attractive.

Left Mk I

Left Mk II

As appreciation for the car grew stronger and more widespread in the very early 1960s, so did admiration for all these qualities. They were sought in all manner of things: mini cameras, ranch rifles, torches and, in particular, all those new electronic gadgets of which the hand-held calculator was the most up to date, with mini radios and mini television sets ever more abundant. With them, all the descriptive prefix 'mini' assured the customer that the notion of 'less is more' could be applied to almost anything. Why not, then, to the skirt?

One thing about the skirt made it different from all those other minithings: it was originally created for the use of the young; for the delight of the young; for the glorification of the young. As with the car itself, its real salvation came from the enthusiasm with which it was taken up by the young.

Below

The Beatles, '63

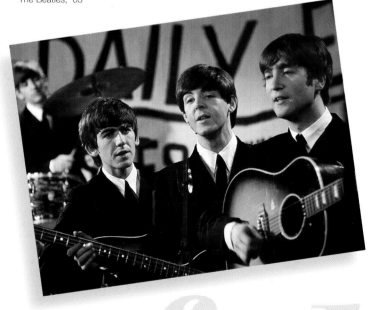

What has been called the Youth Revolution was already under way in the 1950s. Each generation has a tendency to turn against its parents, but the generation growing up after the end of the Second World War had perhaps particular justification for doing so, and there was a very marked break between the generations in that decade. The Beat movement then originating in California ('beat' meant exhausted and defeated – overtones of musical rhythm or beatific drug-induced experiences were later accretions) served well enough to argue a need for overthrowing the previous standards and assumptions of society; but it led only inward and could not last. Much more positive was the assertion by the fifteen-to-twenty age group of its independence.

The change in their situation had many causes – notably the massive redistribution of earnings to the advantage of the young in the consumer society – and they quickly acquired a privileged niche. The increased mobility they enjoyed as a result of the devolution of the motor vehicle played no small part in making their cause secure.

Any political undertones in the youth movement were skillfully side-stepped by the authorities, who saw that the pursuit of pleasure would keep the revolutionary young busy until any political fervour had had time to fade. What might have been an ideological revolt became instead a cultural rebellion, manifest in the music of the Beatles and the Rolling Stones and their kind, in a new scorn for the establishment and a growing respect for the idea of meritocracy. None of them saw in the success of the 'self-made man' the ravages of unskilled labour; the hope of every yet unfulfilled youth was nurtured by a romantic approval of those who had 'made it'.

Below Models sporting the
fashionable 60s 'mini' look

Most manifestly of all, the ideals of the new youth were expressed in clothes. Young people set out deliberately, idealistically, to violate the canons of 'good taste'. They wore clothes that their parents could not wear without looking disastrous or at least ridiculous. Their new spending power killed 'the little dressmaker' stone dead: young people could buy off the peg, ready to wear and to discard in favour of the next fashion of the moment. This was when we truly recognized the truth of what Coco Chanel had said so much earlier: 'Fashion is what goes out of fashion'.

Young people loathed the idea of the formal clothes worn by their elders; the suits and costumes that they saw as a kind of mind-numbing uniform. Ironically, they found their own. The uniform of the young, in time to become the uniform of everybody who did not recognize the nature of uniform, was blue denim trousers, which had come from the USA to become the sensation of the 1950s. What was worn with them, or instead of them, was now sought in a new kind of shop, the boutiques that promised small-scale individuality and nonconformity. One of the most significant was opened in London in 1955 (just one year before John Osborne's *Look Back In Anger* made Britain aware of its angry young men) by a 23-year-old designer who had studied at Goldsmith's College of Art, designed hats for the Danish milliner Erik, and had already made herself a name in cosmetics.

Above Bizarre
Below '62 Miss Italy riding sidesaddle in the genteel Italian manner

Right Twiggy –
the look of the generation

In partnership with her husband-to-be Alex Plunkett Greene, Mary Quant opened her first Bazaar. It was in London, in the King's Road (her first set of styling was to be known as 'the Chelsea look'), and it catered exclusively for 'newly emerged, independent and high-spirited youth'. They were to have a style of their own, essentially unconventional. Tight pants contrasted with sloppy sweaters; girls' thick-knitted stockings might be worn with abbreviated skirts, or with knickerbockers. Denim was supplemented by vinyl, by utility fabrics, and then (practically simultaneous with the Mini) the new man-made fibres, especially stretchy ones such as Crimplene.

'Bliss was it in that dawn to be alive
But to be young was very heaven'
and if you were a young woman the prospects looked even more appealing. Women had tended not to return to the kitchen after the war, and their daughters wanted to move on to a completely new world. Girls rode Lambretta and Vespa scooters as demonstratively as the lads. Fashion models were posed in deliberately 'unladylike' stances. Fashion photographers discovered how much more responsive to lighting were the skinny frail-looking types than their more pneumatic predecessors in the modelling business. 'Little girls with naughty miniskirts and unlikely hair' were the new look, personified by Twiggy – lots of leg, scarcely any breasts, and apparently no underclothes. Young men's trousers were cut to give emphasis to a bulging crotch, and young women's to confirm that the centre of levity corresponded closely to the centre of gravity, all in accordance with fashion historian James Laver's theory of the shifting erogenous zone. Did the miniskirt, asked would-be authoritarians, encourage promiscuity?

Below
Dancing *The Zizzle*, '63

In truth it did not, and never did, need any encouragement. What facilitated it was the disappearance of that discipline learnt from our fathers by precept and our mothers by example, whipped up by Church and school and government and business to their many and several purposes, that could be identified as guilt. The young people of what were sometimes called the Swinging Sixties but were more accurately known as the Permissive Sixties (the effect of which lasted well into the Seventies) dismissed guilt as an ill-founded and undesirable imposition on their freedom to do what seemed natural. If there was a new equality in marriage, there was a new egality outside it: where once the motto of the Family Planning Association had been 'If the cap fits, wear it', contraception had made huge strides. By 1960 in the USA, and 1961 in Britain, the contraceptive pill was on the market, and such sighs as might be heard emanating from the unlikeliest of places (the back seat of a Mini was far from being the most unlikely) were as much of relief as of passion.

Above Uri Gagarin

What a fissile time that was! In 1961 we acknowledged Yuri Gagarin as the first man in space, Ghermin Titov as the next. We flocked to the first disco in London, went into raptures over Mary Quant's second Bazaar, in Knightsbridge, this time (within five years she would have a worldwide business of multimillion-dollar proportions). We worried about the invasion at the Bay of Pigs in Cuba; about the summary erection of the Berlin Wall, ideologically partitioning Berlin; but we went into raptures about Leonard Bernstein's portrayal of ethnic divisions in New York in the film version of the hit musical *West Side Story*. On the London stage, four Oxbridge graduates too young to remember the war set about debunking it – and much else among the politico-religious sacred cows of the English establishment – in an irreverent revue that went *Beyond the Fringe*.

YOU DON'T NEED A BIG ONE TO BE HAPPY

1275 GT

HAPPINESS IS SHAPED

Mini
From Austin Morris with Supercover.
Mini is a registered trade mark

Austin Morris, a subsidiary of BL Cars

Left All the new sex
manuals were saying so

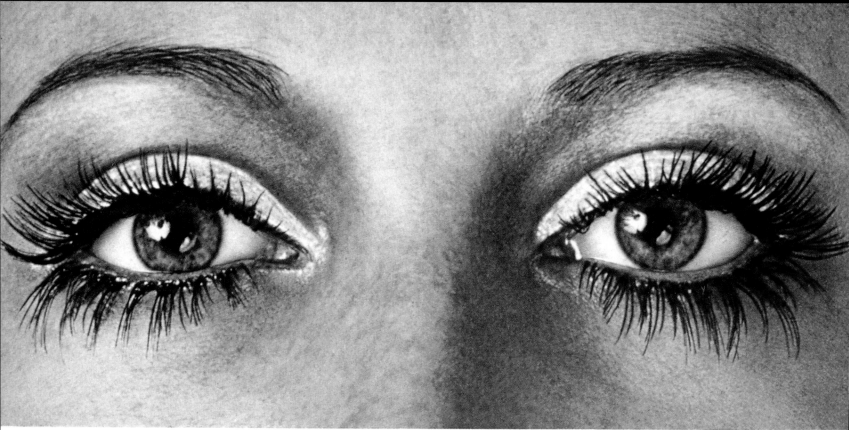

MARY QUANT WILL GIVE YOU A LOVELY PAIR OF SHINERS

Eye Gloss.
Shiny, gleaming. But totally non-greasy.
In moss, blue, grape, beige,
cream. And translucent pearl.
Mary Quant's high gloss
Eye Gloss.

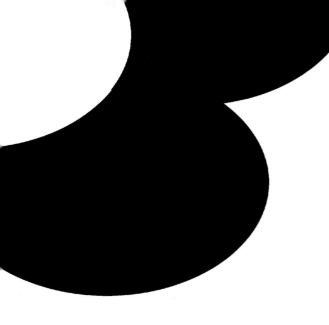

Below Mary Quant and
Vidal Sassoon

Irreverence! That was it, and maybe all there was to it. Break all the rules! Fashion was for everyone, not only for the pampered world of such *hauts couturiers* as Worth, Dior or his successor, Yves Saint Laurent. It was not for the privileged. Be outrageous! If clothes were brief, they were also simple, unadorned, slim (which kept them affordable), and perhaps a little inspired by current notions in science fiction – a burgeoning genre that allowed readers to escape from reality. Clothes had hard edges; hair styles (led by Vidal Sassoon creating the bob in 1963) were geometric and minimalist. Cosmetics favoured black eye make-up, white lipstick. And nothing was made, nor expected, to last.

It was acknowledged (no less enthusiastically in Paris than in London) as the classless car, the one and only car to transcend class barriers. These barriers were self-imposed by people who found some attitudes hard to shed: the people who felt less need to worry after learning that Issigonis had driven Her Majesty the Queen around Windsor Great Park in a Mini. All the car demanded was a receptive attitude, a willingness to see what was wanted and what was superfluous; to recognize that there was much we might do well to forget and much more that we should set ourselves to learn. As Peter Sellers put it, 'The Mini was part of growing up.'

Could any state of mind more receptively admit the minimalist, irreverent, affordable car that was already known – with entire disregard of its Austin or Morris lineage – as the Mini? Could any car better fit the mood of the time, and of the newly enlarged car-buying public, than the Mini? When it first appeared in 1959, the public was baffled; in 1960, people were still diffident. The car was teetering on the brink of failure – and suddenly it was recognized that the Mini was not just a car; was more than a fashion statement; was indeed a whole new way of life. It was a life founded on new freedoms of thought, of expression, of movement; and no less on new freedoms from discipline, from regimentation, and perhaps above all from classification.

Along with the customers, the sales figures grew too. The Mini was undoubtedly a fashion statement, and that was enough to make it popular with all those who were conscious of fashion, perhaps even in thrall to it. The Mini was something greater, however, for it was not in itself confined by fashion: Issigonis, the arch anti-stylist, refused to let anything but function shape the Mini, and thus made that little car the best lesson the world has ever had about the transience and triviality of fashion in contrast to the lasting respect for form as a direct expression of function.

Despite this, there were still some pockets of resistance, some sadly struggling surveyors of the rails on which they ran, blind to the world to which they could not lift their eyes. Some of them were in the marketplace, complaining; others were in BMC, hoping to cash in on memories that were fading, and on names that had been engulfed by the takeovers and mergers that had resulted in the BMC. They were the people for whom the name of Riley or of Wolseley was a memento of what had seemed safe, secure days when chromium and leather and polished wood were evidence of property and propriety.

Right Inside the Elf
Below Outside it

The motto of the Riley had proclaimed the brand 'As old as the industry, as modern as the hour', but in fact the antecedents of the Wolseley were older, dating back to the Wolseley Sheep-Shearing Machine Company Ltd, whose general manager was none other than Herbert Austin. After a few fairly tentative designs, he set the company on the road to elegance and high performance with some dashing (and technically sound) cars, one of which was in its brief time the fastest British protagonist in the Gordon Bennett races. His directors did not share some of his views, and he went off to found his own firm, while Wolseley cars settled into a comfortable rut of respectable middle-class touring cars, making such concessions to fashion and engineering as the times might seem to dictate. This was even more the case after the firm, bankrupt by 1927, had been taken over by Morris, whose own designs formed the basis of more expensive Wolseley variants.

William Morris, born the son of a farm labourer, was made a baronet in 1929, a baron in 1934, and became Viscount Nuffield in 1938. That was the year in which his organization acquired the financially insecure Riley company, which was born at the turn of the century, and had for the last dozen years been making cars with a reputation for being sprightly, even downright sporty. Riley cars did well in competition, and their engines (based, as all future Riley engines would be until 1957, on the original 1100cc four-cylinder machine of 1926-7) had their efficiency exploited in numerous other racing machines, most notably the ERA. After Nuffield took over, though, there was an increasing tendency to make the Riley nothing more than a slightly crisper version of some current Wolseley.

Such were the antecedents of the Riley Elf and the Wolseley Hornet, two versions of the Mini that BMC offered in late 1961 in an effort not only to revive and sustain the selling power of the abandoned brand names but also to appeal to those small-minded snobs who found the idea of a Mini intriguing but the name of Austin or Morris offensive and the evidence of austerity embarrassing. According to the perceptions of the BMC marketing men, the Riley should be slightly the more up-market of the two, but the treatment of both was much the same.

Right The Wolseley
Hornet with Crayford
Convertible body

Almost as necessary to the image was a 'proper' luggage boot, signifying that as a person of property one had some substantial luggage. Unlike the bottom-hinged flap of the regular Mini, which could be left open if what was being carried could survive rain and thieves, the boot lid was hinged at the top, but the bulge allowed the things within to be stored in comparable volume and, what mattered more, in decent privacy.

First and foremost there had to be, as a matter of urgent identification, a traditional, recognizable 'radiator' at the front. It hung like a huge and solitary tooth from the front edge of the bonnet, where it made access to the engine compartment at best awkward and at worst conducive to scalp wounds. It was also a couple of feet away from where the 'radiator' heat-exchanger actually was, over to the side, adjacent to the left front wheel-arch. Never mind; it proudly proclaimed the unique and inimitable Riley (or Wolseley, as the case might be), and the owner would take great pleasure in owning a 'proper' bourgeois car instead of one of those rat-pack Mini contraptions.

Flanking this protrusion were tail fins. Imagine: here was a heavyweight and therefore slower version of a simple little car that could barely manage 72 mph, and to it were being applied the styling features appropriate to something sleeker and much faster. The Americans had used extravagant tail fins, in emulation of ideas culled from aviation, on their big domestic cars since the late 1940s; a few Le Mans specialists, particularly among the French entrants, used them to provide aerodynamic stability for racing sports cars; Bristol, the mighty aeroplane company, began to use fins for their aerodynamic virtues on their

404 and 405 models, new in 1954 and 1955 respectively. But on a Mini? What could they achieve, other than the impression of a piggy bank that had suffered an unfortunate accident?

There were other accretions, outside and inside. The bumpers were heftier, stronger, more like those to be seen on the bigger BMC cars. There was proper leather upholstery and trim (which was not at all to be decried, as anyone with memories of Rexine 'leathercloth' should agree), superior carpeting – the original, basic Mini had been issued with a sensible rubber floor – and full-width walnut surfacing the fascia, with glove-lockers at each extremity in the Riley. There was a lot of chromium. There was even a lid for the ashtray.

A number of changes were to come to the entire Mini range: Moulton's Hydrolastic suspension in 1964; wind-down windows and internalized door-hinges in 1966. Not until 1969 were these two *Prunkwägen* withdrawn; they may have done some good in the time they were on the market, if only by leading unlikely customers to an appreciation of the true Mini virtues. The market took only 60,000 of them.

By 1969, the total output of Minis worldwide was two million. The young and irreverent and the sporting, no less than the motoring purists, despised Elf and Hornet alike, though most of them probably never knew the pre-war cars that bore those names with at least some ring of authenticity. It was the pure and the simple Mini – and in many cases, triggered by the success of the Cooper series in competition, the quick Mini – that truly appealed to all and sundry.

Below

Hydrolastic plumbing

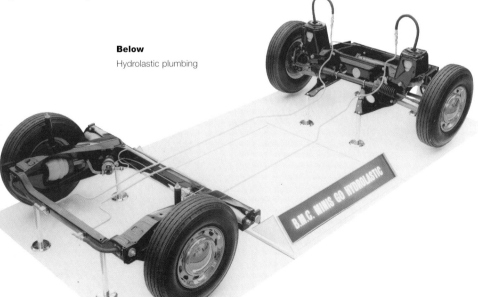

2,000,000ᵀʰ MINI

MINI

The year 1965 was proclaimed *The Year of the Mini* when John Bates designed 'the smallest dress in the world' and the mini-skirt became popular all over the world. What was true of fashion, as a product of youth's cultural revolution, was true alike of cars. The Mini did not so much violate the canons of good taste as set them aside for the devalued things they were. It was (though not for much longer) a car that your parents could not use without appearing ridiculous or even disastrous. It was cheap off-the-peg viability for everyone, not just the privileged, in a time when the idea of the 'throwaway society' was beginning to look attractive. It was, in the words of the Bazaar manifesto, 'for the newly emerged and high-spirited'.

In 1988 Mary Quant had one. Ten years later, David Bowie had one. Twenty or more years earlier, George Harrison – then reckoned one of the thousand best guitarists in Britain and, more to the point, the most proficient musician in the Beatles – had one, as did Ringo Starr and Paul McCartney. Lord Snowdon, probably one of the thousand best photographers in Britain (not that it mattered), had one, with a wind-up window on his side and the sliding type on the other, where the draught would less disturb Princess Margaret's hair.

Above

Is that your car, sir?
Ringo Starr makes a furtive approach after the '64 Monte Carlo Rally

Right
Room for cot and nanny:
Prince Charles' birthday
present for Princess
Diana, '82

Left The Mini Designer:
2000 were made of this
special edition in June 1988.
Designed by Mary Quant, the
interior featured zebra-striped
seats with red seat belts

Left Christine Keeler, '63

Left Paul McCartney, '64

Left Peter Sellers, '64

If pop idols had Minis, then pop fans had Minis, as a matter of course. As for pop, so for jazz, where bandleader Chris Barber (a proficient racing driver who was practically as fast as anyone in a Lotus Type 14 Elite) had one. And if music and images figured in the Mini market, so did the word: Spike Milligan had one. Peter Sellers had more than one. Anyone who was fashionable was likely to have one; anyone who sought to be fashionable might well feel the need for one. No popular cult was without one; but it did not stop there. We might decently suppose that Karim al-Hussain Shah, the fourth Aga Khan, did not buy his in order to make any kind of fashion statement; but perhaps, seeing that he was a twenty-year-old Harvard student when he succeeded his grandfather to the title in 1957, he was glad of a rare opportunity to indulge or proclaim his youthfulness.

Right
Cliff Richard – don't ask!

Left How many?

Above How many more?

BMC, whose public-relations department was in those days staffed by some very able practitioners, missed no opportunity to appeal to the young and high-spirited. One of their most popular promotions was a series of competitions to see how many people could be crammed into a Mini, the inference being that the inevitably intimate physical proximity was very much in the spirit of the times. There is a widespread belief that the maximum number ever achieved was 24, but a riddle then going the rounds had another answer: How many people can you get in a Mini? Seventy-one – two in the front and *soixante-neuf* in the back.

The fun could not last. People grow up, and/or grow dull, and their successors seek change for its own sake. After ten or a dozen years of madness and euphoria, the Mini began to lose its status as a 'pop' icon, began to be bought for its utility by the very same matter-of-fact, price-conscious people for whom it had originally been intended. Few were the customers who saw that it was still without equal as a fashion statement, but they were catered for by a bewildering series of Special Editions that served their purposes while suffering scorn from everybody else.

"As a matter of fact, this *isn't* my favourite car of all time."

"This is one of the latest Minis.®
"My all-time favourite was a Mini I bought a few years back. It was tremendous fun. So much so, I got another.
"But I thought you could never recapture the thrill of your first Mini. Until I saw this one.
"They've put in new wall-to-wall carpets, soundproofing, new seats and controls, a new, smooth suspension and they've

given it Supercover protection.
"My favourite car of all time will always be my first Mini.
"If your next Mini's your first, you'll soon see what I mean!".

Twiggy

Welcome back to a better Mini.

 **Mini**

From Leyland Cars. With Supercover.

Right Riding high

The Special Edition is a marketing device. A basically standard car is tricked out, tarted up, tastefully embellished – choose your own terminology – with a special paint job, extra brightwork, unusual interior trim, fancy wheels and such other trinkets as the tastes of the time suggest. It is produced as a limited edition; the actual number may be determined in advance or found by experience. It is sold either with a small premium or, when sales need a particularly sharp spur, at the normal price. It is meant to turn heads, and with any luck tip the balance in favour of a sale where otherwise no sale might be made. Four million Minis had been made before the first Special Edition seemed necessary in 1976; only after 1981, when annual production dropped to five figures for the first time since 1959, did they begin to come thick and fast.

There were floral ones, ornate ones, others inspired by golf or tennis. Some suggested the sobriety of the City of London, others the smartest purlieus (Chelsea, Piccadilly, Park Lane, Mayfair, the Ritz) of the City of Westminster. Themes were as varied as Tahiti or the equinox, robbery (there was a commemoration of *The Italian Job*, though the cars did not look the same as in the film) or racing. More variations commemorated the Mini's birthdays, every five years beginning with the twenty-fifth, and presumably to be continued. Sometimes it was a matter of a few hundred, sometimes a few thousand, but they were never too numerous. You could always tell which one was yours in the car park.

Above Hot Rod interior
Right The Mini Hot Rod, with its 16-valve, twin-cam 1380cc 160 horsepower engine is claimed to be the fastest accelerating road-going Mini

THE NEW LIMITED EDITION MINI!
FREE ORIGINAL SOUL AND CHART HITS CASSETTE!
SUPER SONY WALKMAN OFFER!

Red Hot
HOT STUFF FOR COLD NIGHTS

Below 1500 special edition Mini Chelseas were made in January 1986

Below left Available in black only, the special edition Mini Park Lane hit the streets in January 1987

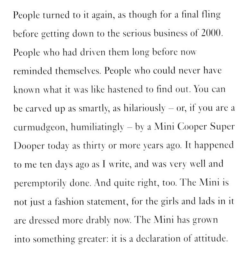

The public attitude to the Mini changed in the 1990s. With a new millennium in sight, people everywhere began to feel a nostalgia for the past; a desire to enjoy again those things that they had enjoyed before time and novelties put them on the shelf or in the bin. Retrospective styling infected everything from motorcycles to radios, and cars were no exception. In particular, the Mini was not, could not be, an exception: it was essentially still as it had always been, thanks to the pure-minded objectivity of its designer. It was neither retrospective nor retrograde; it was the living past.

People turned to it again, as though for a final fling before getting down to the serious business of 2000. People who had driven them long before now reminded themselves. People who could never have known what it was like hastened to find out. You can be carved up as smartly, as hilariously – or, if you are a curmudgeon, humiliatingly – by a Mini Cooper Super Dooper today as thirty or more years ago. It happened to me ten days ago as I write, and was very well and peremptorily done. And quite right, too. The Mini is not just a fashion statement, for the girls and lads in it are dressed more drably now. The Mini has grown into something greater: it is a declaration of attitude.

Above and top
In July 1994, celebrating the 30th anniversary of the Mini's first Monte Carlo rally win, 200 of these cars were built. It was one of the most stunning and collectable Mini special editions ever made

Not just a fashion statement... a declaration of attitude.

Below and right

The Paul Smith limited edition Mini features handmade enamelled gold-plated badges on the bonnet and a black leather interior. When choosing the unique blue for the coachwork, Paul Smith pointed to his shirt and said, 'I want it like this', handing over a square of cloth from his shirt tail

'I had one of the first and this tiny, yet roomy car was

a revelation for handling and driving pleasure. I did

a huge mileage in two years and managed to have a

spectacular accident, rolling sideways and end on.

I escaped through the sliding window. My wife and I

went on honeymoon in it three days later.'

ROY AXE designer for Rover

alternative
enduring
practical
Workhorse
versatile

It is just a car, isn't it? For going to work, shopping, fetching the kids, visiting the patients, carrying parcels, mobilizing the troops, running the farm, parking in the cracks in the kerbstones...?

If the Mini were just a car, it would not have remained in production for forty years, would not have shattered all the illusions of the racing fraternity, might not have inspired new fashions, might not have provoked new driving techniques, might not have added a new word to the language. The Mini was more than just a car, for it was in so many ways extraordinary. Yet, had it not been effective as an ordinary car is expected to be effective, it could not have become all the other things it did. It had to be effective for going to work, shopping, fetching the kids, and all the rest of it.

Left The Countryman was spacious

Left The little Pick-Up made huge sense

69

At first it seemed improbable that the Mini should serve as a jack of all trades. As originally conceived, it had to be a proper car if it were to scupper all the bubble cars and motorized microbes that so offended the likes of Lord. On the other hand, it had to be a miniature car, as tiny as the most grudging perception of utility would allow, and that seemed a huge limitation. Runabout, yes. Jack of all trades? Not a hope.

That was when it was conceived. By the time it was on the roads, hope began to glimmer. Life on the roads was not what it used to be. Traffic was thickening; the population was growing; parking space was dwindling. In 1961 there were 790 people for every square mile of England and Wales, and most of them did not have a garage. The railways were so grossly inefficient that in 1960 Dr Richard Beeching, as head of the British Railways Board, decided that the only solution was extensive closures of lines and stations all over the land. The railways which had once cobwebbed Britain were no longer a practical means of transport for everyday people, and the nineteenth-century towns that they had created had since expanded out of all proportion due to the proliferation of the motor car and other forms of road transport in the latter part of the 1950s.

Suburbs had been growing rapidly since the last quarter of the nineteenth century, but it was only after the First World War that what was seen as the disease of urban sprawl became an epidemic. In the twenty years between the end of the First and the start of the Second World War, the built-up area of Greater London had tripled. Provincial towns grew similarly, if not at the same rate, for it was a clear step up the social ladder for the lower middle class and the upper strata of the working class to set up home in a suburban semidetached house. Vast acreages (often arranged along the flanks of major roads in the increasingly familiar blight of 'ribbon development') were covered with a rash of little bow-windowed two-storey boxes, all alike. George Orwell, in *Coming Up For Air*, hated them: 'You know how these streets fester all over the inner-outer suburbs. Always the same. Long, long rows of little semidetached houses ... as much alike as council houses and generally uglier. The stucco front, the creosoted gate, the privet hedge, the green front door. The Laurels, the Myrtles, the Hawthorns, Mon Abri, Mon Repos, Belle Vue ...'

Above Twin taildoors kept the van short
Below The lowness of the Pick-Up platform was an asset

To have a garage attached to such a house was sheer opulence. To rely on buses or trains, as had been the planners' original assumption, would in due course prove to be sheer folly. What every one of these families needed was a car. Could they afford one? Where would they put it when they were not actually driving it?

The outskirts of the towns and cities were spreading as the centres were opened up to speed traffic through. America had room for this; Japan could not even think about it; Britain and Europe had to take desperate measures, with the centres of cities emptied by bombing and the countryside emptied by urbanization. By 1950, 98% of the UK population was confined to 65% of the land area, 40% of the people being jammed into the six biggest conurbations. An eighth of the population of France packed Paris.

Architects and officials found it hard to see what was coming and to cater for it. Britain, where Town and Country Planning had been invented, at last had a uniform system for the whole country with the passing of the 1947 Act, but had already taken the brave step of instituting the New Towns. This vast project was meant to draw off surplus population from ancient urban centres, and at the same time compensate for the devastation from wartime bombing, by creating new, balanced urban communities which were to provide both homes and work. The plan for 29 new towns in Britain began with a dozen (mostly around London, starting with Harlow), and they were created with impressive speed; but halfway through the programme, revisions had to be made to accommodate the car. The architects had reckoned on one garage to every ten dwellings; hastily the ratio had to be adjusted to house five times as many cars.

People were demanding cars, insisting on cars, with a vehemence hitherto unknown. In Britain the number of cars rose by 55% in five years, to reach 5.5 million in 1960. Five more years and the demand would result in an annual production record of 1.87 million; 600,000 would be exported, but still the roads seemed crowded. There was a record traffic jam, too, measuring 35 miles from Torquay to Yarcombe.

Right Towing was another practical possibility

548 RJO

In those early days of expansion, the Mini was not yet established; but people were getting the message that cars ought not to be excessively big. Even in the USA, as a delayed response to the Suez Crisis, what by American standards might be called 'compact' cars were beginning to appear. What the American people wanted, however, was proper full-size cars, and that was what they bought: every year, 2 million

Chevrolets, for instance, the most popular Impala stretching to 17.5 feet in length. Fortunate America, spread far and fast, had room for that sort of thing: in the year of the Mini's birth the USA had 3,500,000 miles of roads. France had 766,000 miles of them, but crowded little Britain had only 191,000 miles of roads and not yet a substantial motorway. It was no place for big cars.

Above The 1959 Chevrolet Impala
Below Ideally nimble for urban duty

Very slowly at first, but at a rate that would soon accelerate, the British began to appreciate the virtues of the ten-foot Mini. Here was a car that could be tucked into a corner of the front garden if there were no garage, into the tiniest of gaps by the kerb if there were no front garden. It was a car that could minnow its way through shoals of traffic; a car that had a better chance of finding a space in which to park in the centre of the suburb, in the factory grounds, or even in the centre of town. It was remarkably cheap; it was encouragingly economical.

Right It would have been true without the distortion
Below ...and this is the truth

It's Mini Magic!

116 BXX

ONLY A MINI FEELS SO BIG INSIDE... PARKS SO SMALL

That's because the bigness is in the proper place—inside! But take a Mini into traffic. Park at a crowded curbside. Suddenly it seems less than lifesize. Marvellously agile. Willing and able to out-manoeuvre any car around. Over 70 m.p.h. when you want it, and up to 50 m.p.g. Four up, in fact, for ½d. a mile a head—including petrol, oil, tyres and servicing. That's magic for you. Mini-magic!

AUSTIN · MORRIS
MINIS
Minis, Super de Luxe Minis, Mini-Coopers, Mini Countryman and Mini Traveller. Prices from £370 (plus £77.12.11 P.T.) Twelve Months' Warranty and backed by B.M.C. Service.

BRITISH MOTOR CORPORATION LIMITED · BIRMINGHAM & OXFORD

Once it had settled into production, the Mini began to spawn offspring. This possibility had been envisaged some time ago, when the notion of sub-frames had arisen as a cure for the stress concentrations in the prototype bodyshells. Such sub-frames, complete with engine and transmission and suspension, could readily be attached to alternative platforms to create other vehicles. The first to succeed was the Minivan.

The body platform for this van gave it nearly ten inches more overall length, and a 4-inch-longer wheelbase. The bodywork itself was even more spartan than that of the basic Mini (ventilation, in the absence of rear side windows, was just

a matter of opening a tiny hatch in the roof), but the double skinning of the floor to redistribute such things as the battery and spare wheel and provide for a quarter-tonne payload (including the driver) in the surprisingly capacious interior ensured that the remarkable structural stiffness of the Mini saloon was not impaired. Stiffer rear spring-rubbers coped with the greater load, so the van when empty always rode tail-high; but in those days nobody bothered much about headlamp alignment. The Ministry of Transport test, designed to deal with the dangers of ramshackle old cars being dangerous on the highway, was introduced as late as 1960, and then applied only to cars ten or more years old.

GOOD SERVICE MEANS MORRIS MINI VAN and PICK-UP

Below The Minivan was a
much-valued asset to many
small tradesmen

The Minivan was a very attractive proposition to commercial fleet-operators. It was lighter and cheaper than the available alternatives, and its unusual layout kept the floor and hence the loading level very conveniently low. The Post Office was an enthusiastic customer, buying versions of the Minivan for mail collection and for mobile engineers. The AA was another, happy to put its patrol men in this utterly practical little holdall rather than on the exposed seat of the traditional motorcycle with sidecar. The armed forces, particularly the army, were also keen; but the Minivan was by no means meant for or sold only to the big fleet-operators (who in any case could drive very hard bargains that pared profit to the bone). It served also to mobilize many a small tradesman.

It was very cheap indeed, because, as a commercial vehicle, it did not attract purchase tax. Many a would-be owner of a Mini saloon began to figure ways and means of making the van version serve his purposes. Some kind of additional seating could easily be tacked in (the front passenger's seat was optional) and, if the occupants did not mind the dark interior, all should be well. There could be no relieving of that darkness by putting windows in the blank side-panels, for HM Customs & Excise would promptly declare the thing a private vehicle and levy tax accordingly. Nor – and this was a point that many missed – could the commercial vehicle legally be driven on the highway at more than thirty mph (forty on the motorway), a regulation that all too many magistrates and police teams joyously enforced. The police themselves made much use of the Minivan – but as always the police were, in practice if not in theory, above the law.

BMC could do nothing to change the laws, but they did what they could to ease the private buyer's lot. A kit was marketed that would convert the Minivan into a capacious, if not exactly comfortable, four-seater. It was as spartan as ever: the price had been kept down, and there was no interior mirror, no carpet, nor anything else much. There were, however, twin doors at the tail – not because they made access to the interior any easier, but because the Minivan needed to be assembled on the regular nose-to-tail production line with its doors open, and this double-door arrangement saved two feet of production-line space behind each van.

Right The interior-furnishing kit made the van habitable, if not exactly comfortable

Above A 1960 Austin Minivan – note the ventilator on the roof

The Minivan came on the scene in 1960. Only a year later there was another commercial Mini on the same platform as the van. This was the Pick-Up (you could hardly add the word 'truck' for something so tiny), and it was an entirely logical development. Behind the front seats a flat panel sealed off the cabin, behind which a load platform ran flat all the way to the fold-down tailgate at the stern. If desired (it later became a standard accessory) a canvas 'tilt' or cover could be draped over a couple of steel hoops to protect the load from the weather, with a transparent-plastic rear screen to complete the enclosure. Production of the Pick-Up barely exceeded 11% of the total half-million and more Minivans that had been built when both ceased in 1983, but that was mainly because the notorious British climate did not encourage the use of such vehicles, however much the type might flourish beneath kindlier skies.

2 ways of giving your business

AUSTIN
mini ¼-ton Pick-up

The slickest and most economical means ever of transporting a 5-cwt. (254-kg.) load! Ingenious design and practical body styling have been successfully co-ordinated to produce this revolutionary runabout, ideally suited to the needs of the smaller business. Such tradesmen as plumbers, builders, painters, or nurserymen will find that within the compact proportions of the Austin Mini ¼-ton Pick-up are approximately 19½ sq. ft. (1·83 m.²) of floor space and a totally enclosed cab with saloon car comfort for two people. A canvas tilt cover is also available, at extra cost, should it be necessary to protect a consignment against adverse weather.

that 'up-to-date' look

AUSTIN
mini

Below The Pick-Up sporting its canvas protective cover

All photos

The versatility of the 'Woody'

AUSTIN se7en *Countryman*

....for pleasure

Here's the latest newcomer from Austin of England! The Austin Seven Countryman— revolutionary in concept, it is smart in appearance, dependable and economical to operate in either of its dual-purpose categories.
As a passenger carrying vehicle, this brilliant new Countryman can be favourably compared to a saloon car in every sense of the word. Fully equipped to de luxe specification, it has all the motoring refinements so necessary for the pleasurable convenience of the modern family.

Other peculiarly British tastes and prejudices were addressed with estate-car versions of the Mini, embodying the lengthened floorpan of the van. In their simplest forms, the Austin Seven Countryman and the Morris Mini-Traveller were little more than windowed versions of the Minivan; but that little was calculated to indulge British notions of civilisation. Carpets, a headlining, profuse trimming (extending even to the petrol tank in the tail) and other touches of

what in the context might be thought luxury all added up to about 110 lb extra weight to be carried. On the other hand, luggage (or load) space was far greater than in the regular Mini saloon, so there was much practical appeal in this essentially workaday expression of a vehicle concept that had in Britain been traditionally rather posh. To increase the snob appeal even further, the marketing department decided to literally batten additional woodwork on to the exterior, decreeing that the gentry had a right to expect proper visible timberwork. On other BMC estate cars, especially the Morris Minor Traveller, such woodwork did in fact play a structural part in the bodywork; but the Countryman and Traveller had no need of any such stiffening, and the pieces of wood were simply glued on to the flanks and rear doors. The effect was quite ludicrous, and poor Issigonis was enraged by its hypocrisy and pretension.

MORRIS MINI-TRAVELLER

Below One of Broadspeed's specialities has been the custom creation of retro-styled Minis, often with up-to-date features that would have been beyond the ambitions of the times being evoked. The picture in the centre shows Mr and Mrs Roy E. Disney of Burbank, California, taking delivery of their newly restored Mini Cooper S Countryman from the Broadspeed premises in Suffolk. The retro-Woody Countryman is created by restoring an original 1960s Mini Countryman, incorporating panels and components from new Mini Coopers

Above The Mini
Clubman estate

Not everything about the 'Woody' Mini was bad, however: the lateral windows which lit the capacious rear compartment were of the sliding type, enabling the occupants to enjoy lots of ventilation. Nor did the top speed suffer greatly from the additions, dropping only a trifle to 69 mph; but the great increase in weight was crippling. Other Minis, according to their kind, could accelerate; the estate versions could at best be said to gather speed.

Luckily, it did not matter a great deal for the most popular use to which the estate was put: as a shopping car of unrivalled convenience. It mattered little more for what seemed to be the little wagon's next most popular employment: as a vehicle for carrying a dog. This rather utilitarian career was duly recognized when, in 1962, BMC offered a plain metal estate without the mock-Tudor trimmings.

In the days after BMC became British Leyland, in the days of the Mk 3 Mini, the Clubman estate took over. The wood of the old Woody had at least been real wood, superfluous though it was; the wood of the Clubman estate was fake wood. At a time when it was being said of interior trim in up-market saloons that the British could make plastics look like wood, the Germans could make wood look like plastics, and the Italians would make anything look like plastics, the pride of the Clubman estate was the shame of the polymer industry. Only in 1977, and under the pressure of something that was more probably penury than honesty, the trashy trappings gave way to mere painted lines.

Right The Mini
Clubman estate, post
1977, featuring painted
lines rather than the
fake wood

'Moke' is a nineteenth-century term, used by Australians to describe a horse of low quality and by the English to denote a donkey. Around 1962 this term became the name given to the most uncompromisingly basic of all Minis, one that had been in gestation longer than the Mini itself.

When he was working at Morris during the war, Issigonis had been involved in a series of jobs on military vehicles. One that he himself designed was a miniature tank, or more correctly scout car, known as the Salamander. It had front-wheel drive with double-wishbone suspension, as would the Mini; it was sprung by torsion bars, as was the front of the Morris Minor; and it had a monocoque hull, as would most cars in due course. It had nothing of the aura of America's heroic Willys Jeep, but Issigonis was very aware of the need for a lightweight version of just such a general-purpose military car.

Ideally it should be so small and light that it could easily be packed flat into an aircraft, parachuted into the scene of action, and deployed more or less instantly. The Royal Navy had just the thing in post-war years, a pick-up version of the redoubtable Citroën 2CV: assembled in Slough specifically for the Admiralty, this enduring little vehicle could be lifted by helicopter and dropped ashore for operations that might well face rough terrain. The duration of the contract with Citroën was coming to an end, however, so there was cause for BMC to think that a substantial market might be found for a new substitute.

The prototypes proferred by BMC were sadly inadequate. The proposed military vehicle had a pressed steel platform base graced with Mini suspension and a driveline incorporating the original 948cc engine. It weighed only about 300 lb, could be stacked on top of another – and perhaps another – and that was all the good to be said of it.

The ground clearance was too small for rough country. The promoters suggested, rather impractically, that in those circumstances the four soldiers normally travelling in it could pick it up and carry it – along with their weapons and emergency rations. On top of this, the weight distribution with soldiers aboard unloaded the front tyres too much for uphill traction. Nor did the shape of the basic airborne flat-pack encourage a stable parachute fall. Nor was the buckboard durable enough.

By 1962 Issigonis had come up with something more sophisticated. A proper Mini floorpan, somewhat abbreviated in wheelbase, now carried the machinery. The ride height was increased and a sump guard placed beneath the engine. The War Office was not impressed. Issigonis then plugged another engine, an 850, into the rear of the vehicle so as to ensure ample four-wheel-drive traction and stimulating performance. The War Office remained unimpressed.

Right Even a Moke
can look tidy alongside
a Helicopter
Below Absence of
doors makes airfield
duties easier

Left Note the absence
of snow piled up in front
Below Despite its
panache, the War Office
remained unimpressed

Could the civilian market be tempted instead? The wheelbase reverted to normal; a simple open-platform chassis made use of big boxed sills to make it suitably stiff and strong; and the rest of the simple steel body was designed to enhance the military-utility impression that was sought – even to the use of a very military-looking spruce green for the paint.

Did the civilians want it? Unfortunately not! Even with the canvas tilt erected, even with the optional extra windscreen wiper, it was hardly the sort of recreational vehicle that could be reconciled with the reality of British weather. As a commercial vehicle it came cheap, at as little as £405 and without tax; but, when it was reclassified as a passenger car in 1967, even this advantage disappeared.

The Moke did not altogether disappear. One of the lessons learnt by people in the 1960s was the importance of mixing business with pleasure, that if you did not enjoy what you were doing you would not do it well. For those few whom it suited, the Moke suited the principle very well. People who needed to be seen if they were to be employed, people to whom exposure meant publicity rather than hypothermia, found cause to be seen in Mokes. The little minijeep conveyed just the right impression for them, with all the irreverent insouciance of the Mini saloon and all the pleasant astonishment of the open – *entirely* open, from the ankles up – car. In some parts of the world, such people might be golfers or beach-loafers; but, where the names were being dropped and reputations hoisted, they were likely to be artists, designers, models, photographers.

Right The updated Moke, made in Australia

Right A mob of photographers clamour to photograph the winner of the 'Miss World' beauty contest, after the competition in London in November 1966

Photography, the trade that had once meant sycophancy with a Leica, had been seized and shaken by a bunch of East End lads, Cockneys either real or pretend ('camp Cockney' was the new lingua franca of the graphics trade, as it was to be in the theatre, on the radio, and elsewhere). They had gravitated to the King's Road in London and levitated to stardom in the most starry-eyed career of the 1960s. With miniature cameras (the day of the single-lens reflex had arrived: *every* motor-racing photographer of the 60s had to use an Asahi Pentax unless he wanted to be viewed with grave suspicion) and giant tripods – declaring respectively faith and doubt – with ever bulkier bags of apparatus burdening their shoulders, photographers lucky enough to be working in agreeable conditions found it more than a little convenient to be working from the deck of a Moke.

Harri Peccinotti was one of them. An art director whose impatience with photographers had prompted him to become a photographer himself, he had been selected to shoot the pictures that would make the 1968 Pirelli calendar. Under the inspired direction of Derek Forsyth, this publicist's gem somehow managed to capture the spirit of the 1960s without shackling itself to any limiting manifesto.

Love poetry was the theme of that year's calendar. Love poems were found, from Ronsard to Ginsberg, from Japan to London, and Harri Peccinotti was given the task of evoking the words. Off he went, with Forsyth and the girls and the assistants and a Moke, to the desert beaches of Tunisia.

The beaches were not quite deserted. In an Islamic country where women covered themselves from eye and camera alike, the models always came under surveillance whenever they uncovered themselves for a picture. Worse was to come: as tension between Israel and the Arab states grew, Americans were being ordered out of Libya, and with only one suitcase each. The day after Jim Clark won the Dutch GP with the new Lotus 47, the Six Days' War erupted in Israel. Arab suspicions of Americans and Englishmen abroad grew serious. For men with pictures of uncovered women; a trunk full of cartridge belts (some of the poems, eventually unused, were about the Mexican revolution); and a desert vehicle, a vehicle with obvious military potential, a Moke, it was a disaster.

It did not help Peccinotti, the first to leave, that the keys to the Moke had been lost. He spent a morning digging in the river of sand which ran beneath their wattle huts, found the keys, and set off. The desert sand slowed the Moke, so that the dogs from a local Touareg settlement gave him a hard run. Imagining they were lions, he beat them off with a water bottle. In Tunis he was arrested. Derek Forsyth was, elsewhere, stopped and questioned; but there was still Rodney Kinsman, husband of one of the models, who had a direct air ticket from Djerba to London. Forsyth had gambled on giving Kinsman nearly all the film, and he managed to bring it home without questions. The calendar was saved; the Moke was lost.

Above A Mini Moke cram?

Left Made in Portugal,
the 'Californian Moke'

Top and above By 1994, the
Mini Moke SE could look smart

The Moke looked like a dead loss to its makers, too. Fewer than 15,000 had been built, and only about a tenth of those had been sold in the UK. In 1968, production in Britain was stopped. Down under in Australia, though, the Moke had already been in production in BMC's Sydney factory, and it would continue; in Australia, the Moke was quite a success. It was given the more sensible 1000cc engine, and later it enjoyed thirteen-inch wheels, better brakes, better cooling. Later still, Sydney evolved the 1300cc Californian version with quite a few fancy extras, then a pick-up version; later still came a smart new hood, a bit better than a mere tilt, that could be closed with zip fasteners. When finally in 1981 Moke production in Australia was stopped, 26,000 had been built and sold.

Still the donkey was not dead. A year earlier, assembly of Moke parts from Australia had begun in Portugal. It reverted to twelve-inch wheels as part of a rationalization programme to minimize the costs of the exercise, but it remained popular for another 10,000 cars. It was Rover who finally put a stop to it, selling off the rights to the Italian makers of Cagiva motorcycles, who put it into production yet again. It was seen as a stylish, fun car, as indeed it was if your interpretation of the word 'style' was suitably liberal. 'Work' – a four-letter word not overly popular in the 1960s when there was plenty of it about – was no longer at the top of its agenda.

...most responsive, sensible and just plain wonderful

Paul Skilliter, journalist

MINI MOKE

AUSTIN ROVER

'Forget the Golf and Peugeot GTis: this is the car that started the hot hatch craze.'

MARK GILLIES journalist

technique
engineering
dynamics
Racer
safety

The influence of motor racing on motor-car design is not to be denied. Even if racing does not produce hardware for assimilation into the production cars of the manufacturer concerned, even if that manufacturer takes no active part in racing, there is no questioning the importance of the standards that a familiarity with motor racing gives to the designer of a touring car.

To compete is to discover what is possible, and few creative people (such as the best car designers must be) will be content to exploit less than what they know to be possible. Thus the touring car inherits from the racing car, usually at some distance in time, the standards of steering,

Above John Rhodes shows off the 35th Anniversary Edition at Goodwood

roadholding, braking, handling and general controllability (as well perhaps, but not necessarily, the standards of sheer acceleration and speed) with which we identify active safety and much that is taken to represent progress in car engineering.

In the 1990s, when all forms of motoring competition have been so spurred by commercialism, arriving at what looks to contemporary eyes like extremes of artificiality and therefore of irrelevance, there must remain some truth in the above contention. In the 1950s, particularly during the period of the Mini's gestation, the truth was powerfully, almost overwhelmingly, evident.

Left Racing and rallying, the twin aspects of a glorious competition career: John Rhodes making smoke, Makinen's Monte Carlo Rally Mini enjoying its fame, both in 1967

In the championship Grands Prix which represented the pinnacle of motor racing in that decade, the world had passed through what had been seen as a golden age when, under the rules of a formula prescribing engines of no more than 2.5 litres displacement, cars of remarkable variety in design (their engines embraced V8, V6, straight-8, straight-6 and straight 4-cylinder layouts) explored the ultimate reaches of the classical front-engined rear-drive car. Before the decade was out, these had all been overthrown by a new breed of smaller, more agile cars in which, inspired by the example of the Cooper machines which seized the world championship in each of the previous two years of the formula, the engine was located behind the driver. The new levels of dynamic ability then reached did nothing to belittle the achievement of the Mini, which, when it appeared in 1959, displayed an ability to reach cornering forces equal to those of the GP cars of only five years earlier.

Top right 1964 Mini Cooper S at Goodwood in 1993
Bottom right Mini Cooper autocrossing

At that time, the other relevant branch of motoring sport – rallying – was enjoying a great rise in popularity and, with it, perhaps inevitably, a considerable increase in rigour. In many countries, not least in Britain, the idea of speed events conducted on the public highway was difficult enough to accommodate even occasionally, but to have them scouring the countryside every weekend was quite untenable. Instead, rallying had for some time been confined to modest and friendly jaunts in which time-keeping and navigational skills were paramount, speed and driving skills at a discount. There were notable exceptions, the classic Monte Carlo Rally being by far the most notable of all; elsewhere, and particularly in Scandinavia, rallies were being literally sidetracked on to forest paths which called for cars to be ruggedly constructed and to have adroit responses to highly specialized driving techniques. In this light, the great structural stiffness of the Mini hull, and the quickness of its response to driving methods for which front-wheel drive made it most appropriate, gave it a potential that was recognized at birth.

The first competition entered by any Mini was not a public competition at all. It was a private rivalry among motoring journalists who were keen to be the quickest round the main testing circuit (incorporating high-speed banking and the sinuous and hilly 'Snake' section) at the FVRDE (Fighting Vehicles Research and Development Establishment) a couple of dozen miles southwest from London, at Chobham, where the Mini was being introduced to the press (and vice versa) shortly before its public launch. The honours went to Monsieur Paul Frère, a Belgian gentleman who has more successfully than anyone else combined the activities of racing driver and motoring journalist. His right hand has not lost its cunning even today, nor his right foot; but at that time he already had a fine record, not only in single-seaters (he was in the Ferrari F1 team) but also in long-distance sports-car events such as the Reims Twelve Hours, which he won (with his patrician compatriot Olivier Gendebien as co-driver) in 1957 and 1958. Yet, if his performance at Chobham was regarded with some awe, so was that of the Mini.

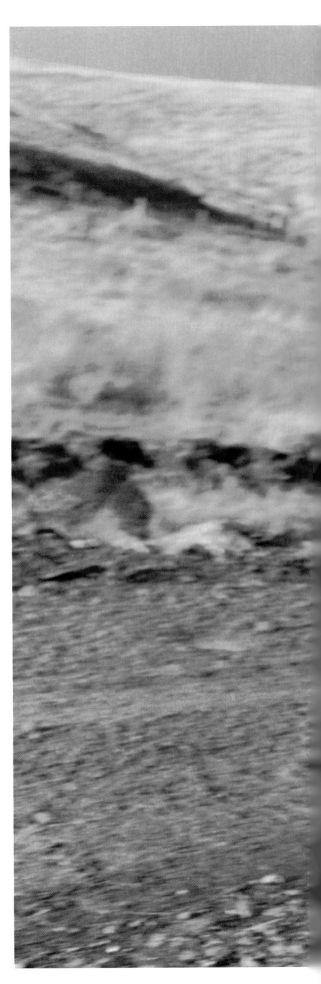

Right Full nose-up
pitch allowed by
Hydrolastic suspension

Nevertheless, popular opinion of the car at the time of its launch was that it was emphatically a utilitarian runabout. It did not have the power that would surely be requisite in a circuit racer, nor the ground clearance that would be no less desirable in a rally car. To some extent, popular opinion was correct: in its earliest days, the Mini was both raced and rallied – more out of curiosity than conviction – and, if it was quicker than might have been expected, it was quickest in demonstrating its obvious limitations. Its unique combination of advantages (the stability, the agility born of rapid responses, the structural stiffness, the minimal size and weight), derived from an equally unique layout, had to be learnt, but the learning curve steepened rapidly as drivers began to understand how the car could be exploited, and also began to explain its qualities to a fast-growing audience of interested parties.

Issigonis himself was not interested in the car's competition potential. The directors of BMC were less sure of themselves, but were inclined to doubt the commercial value of the Mini participating in speed events. They were not without some experience in drawing up profit-and-loss accounts for competition involvement, but they had no idea that the Mini might be as persuasive as it proved to be. Their competitions manager, the renowned Marcus Chambers, was one who did recognize its potential, and did what he could to realize it. Before the year was out, a BMC team of three Minis entered the RAC Rally.

They all failed. Engine oil escaped from a crankshaft bearing into the clutch, which began to slip. The normal fix for such a problem was to squirt a fire-extinguisher into the clutch, but under the stress of competition motoring that was inadequate; in later events the crews even tried stuffing road grit into it, in the hope of summoning friction of some sort.

Engineers distinguish two different kinds of treatments for problems. The 'fix', the immediate palliative, should be merely the first, temporary way of coping with the difficulty. The 'cure', the measure taken to prevent it ever happening again, is usually a long-term project involving alterations to manufacturing procedures or even redesign of the affected parts. In the case of the oil-contaminated clutch, the cure was simply a better (and doubtless more expensive) oil seal between the crankshaft bearing and the clutch housing.

The BMC management began to see the virtues of competition in identifying problems that might otherwise cause some embarrassment when they surfaced in customers' cars, and in facilitating the engineering of both fixes and cures more rapidly than could be managed by the normal hierarchy of the design and development departments. In this spirit, they were persuaded to authorize a BMC team of three Minis to tackle their first international event, the 1960 Monte Carlo Rally. There were three private entrants as well, but the combined assault of six Minis on the event, nearly all of them beset by accidents and other misfortunes, merely resulted in four finishing in places ranging from 23rd to 73rd – not bad, in the circumstances, but not good.

Left The Competition Department workshop at Abingdon

Below Engine bays: Cooper Mk III above 1963 Cooper S

This Mini is not only handing out a lesson. It's learning something too

That's BMC creative engineering

We don't race and rally just for fun. Or just to win. We use the track and the rally circuit as proving-grounds for better engineering ideas.

So while we are winning (and since 1953 BMC have gained more outright, category and class wins in European Championship

Rallies than any other manufacturer in the world!) we are also learning, for sure, how to give you a safer, more efficient and reliable family car.

Test a BMC car yourself. Race it. Rally it. Drive it on roads you know. You'll find the lessons we learn

on the track mean a lot of extra motoring pleasure!

BMC

THE **BRITISH** MOTOR CORPORATION LIMITED
LONGBRIDGE, BIRMINGHAM

AUSTIN · AUSTIN-HEALEY · MG · MORRIS · RILEY · VANDEN PLAS · WOLSELEY

Better was to come. The Mini won its class in the Geneva Rally, did the same in the Alpine Rally, and the same again in the 1961 Tulip Rally. The little car had shown that tiny wheels and negligible ground clearance counted for less than front-wheel drive, a wide track, clever suspension and a well-placed centre of gravity. It had also shown that its poor little brakes were sadly inadequate. Meanwhile, mildly tuned Minis entered in minor races of the kind that took place every weekend in Britain demonstrated that the standard ten-inch wheel was weak: in some cases the centre portion of the wheel was torn right out. When a stronger steel wheel was substituted, it was marked with the MG octagon so that scrutineers might recognize it.

Again, better was to come. While an unholy rabble of backyard tuning firms parted fools from their money for tuning conversions that sometimes made the Mini faster and sometimes made it merely harsher and louder, a more professional outfit known as Downton Engineering was producing real satisfaction for the speed hungry. The proprietor of this firm, Daniel Richmond, was an interesting fellow who dismissed his obviously clever work as merely 'being careful', and affected greater enthusiasm for wine, fishing and good company. One of his friends, as it happened, was Issigonis, who liked to be kept abreast of what was being done to the Mini by outsiders.

There was another friend of Issigonis who was anxious to do very interesting things to it. John Cooper, whose Grand Prix racers won the world championships of 1959 and 1960, may have been smarting a little from the fact that Colin Chapman – the clever and clear-thinking businessman who ran Lotus – was copying the Cooper example with rear-engined racing cars that were actually better than the Coopers. At any rate, John Cooper wanted to find somewhere a small four-seater car that could be made quick and well-behaved enough to outrun the heartrendingly beautiful Lotus Elite coupé on the racing circuits of Britain and mainland Europe. He had tried putting racing machinery into a Renault Dauphine, only to find that the evil handling of that little blighter could not be sufficiently mitigated. When the Mini appeared, Cooper began to wonder whether it was what he had been looking for.

Below Mini Cooper
Mk I, 1961

The engine held no mysteries for him. Cooper had been running a team of Formula Junior cars, which were powered by a version of the BMC A-type engine tuned to deliver 85bhp. He knew about the Mini's hopeless brakes, and knew that Lockheed would be only too happy to prove a point or two by producing a suitably small disc brake for the car. He knew that his henchman Jack Knight made a speciality of gearboxes and could reorganize the transmission of the Mini to advantage. He knew Issigonis. What more could he ask?

While remaining friendly, Issigonis was not sympathetic. As we have noted, he always saw his Mini as a car for the less well-off people who needed a car, and he could not identify the spendthrift extravagance, the grasping, the cheating and the posturing insincerity of the racing world with his ideals. It was not as if he had no experience of competition: he had actually met Cooper when they were both having a go at the speed trials along the sea front at Brighton. Issigonis was driving his prewar Lightweight Special; Cooper was driving his own home-made special, the one that ended by monopolizing the 500cc class in British single-seater racing, the one that first made us aware of the benefits (which Germany's prewar Auto Union GP racer only led us to doubt) of putting the engine behind the driver. At the end of a kilometre from a standing start, Cooper was the quicker.

He and Issigonis had other reasons to meet professionally, for Cooper officially bought the basic engines for his Formula Junior racers from a part of the BMC organization, and Issigonis expected to be kept abreast of development work done by outsiders. For all that, the designer of the Mini could not bring himself to approve Cooper's proposals for a high-performance version, but it seems that he may himself have suggested to Cooper that he go higher up the BMC pyramid, to managing director George Harriman.

The boss listened with interest to what Cooper had to offer, listened with some disbelief to the suggestion that a thousand of these superheated versions could be sold, and finished the interview with a simple order: 'Take a car and do it.' That was all the encouragement Cooper needed.

It was easy to calculate that 55bhp would suffice to make the Mini do 85 mph, which seemed a decent advance beyond the 72 mph of the standard car. It would be a lot less than the 85bhp of a potential Elite-beater, but that proposition was fading in Cooper's mind as he saw the potential for much greater sales of a car that would still be manageable and economical while going respectably fast. In any case, the Lotus Elite, being so shoddily made (although a huge improvement came when Lotus persuaded the plastics division of the Bristol Aeroplane Company to make the glassfibre mouldings

for the body), was proving a sore trial to the customers' patience and would soon be a spent force. What the enthusiast-at-large wanted was an affordable small car that was fast enough, stable and controllable enough to run rings round the more ponderous high-performance cars of the day; to run across country at high average speeds; and to run the gauntlet of urban traffic with such agility that, even in the most trying of circumstances, driving it would be *fun*.

That was exactly the car that John Cooper confected. With a 997cc version of the A-type engine, with higher and closer gear ratios selected by a more positive remote-control gearlever, with disc front brakes and wider tyres, with a colour-contrasted roof and two-tone trim *and* a 100 mph speedometer, the Mini Cooper enjoyed a clamorous welcome when it appeared in September 1961.

Above right The 1962 Monte Carlo Rally: Mabbs pulled Aaltonen out of this

Right *Les Dames* winning their *Coupé* in the 1962 Monte

In the ensuing winter it had its first competition outing, on the 1962 Monte Carlo Rally. Pat Moss (Stirling's sister) and Ann Wisdom (Tom's daughter) shared one, winning the Coupe des Dames. Another Cooper, supported by the works but not an official entry, was shared with established Geoff Mabbs by a newcomer named Rauno Aaltonen. As yet little known but quite prodigious in his ability, Aaltonen brought the car up to second place behind the SAAB of the eventual winner, Erik Carlsson, before crashing on the Col de Turini.

'…but tradition
Approves all forms of
competition'
Arthur Hugh Clough

On rough terrain, regardless of
conditions, the Mini's performance
in rallying is second to none

As a demonstration of what could be done with the Mini, Aaltonen's performance was salutary. As a token of the professionalism with which the newly appointed competitions manager at BMC, Stuart Turner, would in future run the department, it was reassuring. That token was soon validated when the ladies, the Moss-Wisdom pair again, won the 1962 Tulip Rally outright. Before the year was out, three Mini Coopers scooped the team prize in the RAC Rally, with yet another new Finnish name – Timo Makinen, probably the fastest of them all – among the crews. There was only one more star driver to be brought in, Ireland's genial but suavely professional Paddy Hopkirk, who made his Mini debut with skill and with grace, but without much luck, in the 1963 Monte Carlo Rally, when he finished sixth. His luck was to change very soon. So was

Above On the RAC Rally, 1966
Right Timo Makinen, briefly bearded in 1966

that of the works rally team, which had not really scored as well in major events as had been hoped. Minis were doing well in minor events all over the place, in racing as well as in rallying, building a good reputation among clubmen and enthusiasts everywhere; but it is not of such stuff that great publicity is made, and great publicity is what a factory-supported competitions programme is supposed to achieve.

Frankly, the original 997cc Mini Cooper, from 1961 to early 1964, was not of such stuff as a great competitions programme could be made, either. It was by the standards of its time a splendid little road car, capable of averaging higher speeds at lower expense than anything else then generally marketed, and it sold accordingly, to the tune of about 25,000 specimens rather than the 1,000 that John Cooper first envisaged and George Harriman doubted. However, the standards being set in international competition were rising rapidly, under the impulsion of generous spending by the likes of Ford, Renault,

Porsche, Citroën and Mercedes-Benz. There was sometimes help to be sought in such handicapping systems as had been applied since 1961 to the Monte Carlo Rally, where the intention was to favour the 'ordinary' production cars (supposedly in production form, though all manner of tweaks could be performed without arousing the ire of the French scrutineers, who would hound down any infraction of the regulations by an entrant from any other country) that the French liked to enter, as against the more extravagant sporting cars favoured by Germany and Italy.

Right Mini Cooper Mk III

Left John Cooper with the 1991 Mini in the pit lane at Goodwood

This sort of nationalism was not uncommon. There had been in 1959 a notorious Portuguese rally (the first foreign foray for the Mini: two started and two finished, which was progress) in which the leading cars were all disqualified at the end for wearing their numbers in the wrong colour, whereupon some local entrants were pleased to step up and collect the awards. Italy was often hostile to foreigners, especially French and German. Britain contrived to make things difficult for them in a more graceful style, but motoring sport was so strong in Britain at that time, with the overwhelming bulk of the entrants British (if only because of that intervening water beyond Dover's white cliffs), that there could be little cause for resentment if a foreign entrant occasionally prospered.

Be that as it might, the original Mini Cooper had rather too many limitations to be a serious force in international events. Its engine was not really lusty enough, nor amenable to really advanced tuning. Its front brakes, although better than the original puny drums, were too small. It was good, but just not good enough.

Young Stuart Turner, making his indelible mark as the finest competitions manager we ever saw (he was to do it even better for Ford, later on), demanded something better. Issigonis agreed that it was possible and desirable, and this time he wanted to be involved. So did Daniel Richmond, who had been doing some typically Downton work on the racing engines for single-seaters. The work was done quickly, just as soon as the decision had been taken to make the new Mini Cooper a 1100cc job, capable of being shortened to 1000cc or stretched towards 1300cc if competition categories demanded it.

Left 1965 Mini Cooper S looked innocent

Here was an engine of outstanding quality, adapted in all manner of details to run strongly and dependably, to endure severe punishment and still deliver the power that was sought. It was made of the finest materials then available, including a superb super-hardened steel for the crankshaft and a nickel-based valve alloy derived from aviation gas turbines, where conventional steels could not tolerate the combination of thermal and mechanical stress that the turbine blades had to survive. From 1071cc, this engine produced 70bhp with ease, and could do it all day, yet remained flexible and sweet-mannered enough for driving on ordinary roads at ordinary speeds. In a car weighing about 1400 lb it produced much livelier acceleration than the old Cooper, and a higher top speed; and both of these could the more readily be used because the car could now stop as well as it could go.

More substantial brake discs, with a servo in support, could now be fitted at the front, because there were now wider wheels to make room for them, wheels with ventilating holes to provide cooling air for them, wheels carrying the latest sporting radial-ply tyres to ensure grip and response and durability. Quicker steering gear, with only 2.3 turns now required to twirl the steering wheel from lock to lock, offered the driver every chance to exploit those tyres. This, in May 1963, was a true sports car, and the fact was emblazoned on it: this was the Mini Cooper S.

Left Aaltonen and Ambrose, 1st in the 1963 Alpine Rally

It was this handicap classification that earnt all the publicity, and put the Mini firmly on the French map, with orders for the car flooding in even while the event was still running, and further orders for three times the usual number following at the end of the season. If the Mini was to become, as it did, one of the most chic, most cultivated, most status-enhancing fashion accessories in Parisian society, it was in the dealerships of Montpelier during the Tour de France that it first proved its attractions.

Turner pressed the new S into service immediately. Rauno Aaltonen was the talk of the Alpine Rally, leading the touring class from start to finish (there was no overall winner) and winning a coveted Coupe des Alpes for finishing unpenalized. Then came Paddy Hopkirk's rousing performance in the Tour de France, which was a sort of road rally punctuated by speed trials on hills and racing circuits. The touring category looked like the province of big Jaguars and Ford Galaxies, but the Cooper S came third in it, third overall on scratch, and – most important of all, for this was France – first on handicap.

Hopkirk was on top form. At the beginning of 1964, he started from Minsk in the Monte Carlo Rally, accompanied by one of the team's top co-driver navigators, Henry Liddon. They had to fight the opposition, the handicap, the weather, and the hazards of Russian roads, not to mention the chauvinistic fury of a gendarme when Hopkirk wrong-slotted the wrong way into a one-way street somewhere in the depths of France. They survived it all, and they won.

Above Hopkirk and
Liddon signed this 1964
Monte shot
Right The same chaps
at the prize-giving
Below 33 EJB – winner
of the 1964 Monte Carlo
Rally

Below Coming down past the Monaco harbour in 1964

It was a famous victory. Ford had openly proclaimed that they were going to win, had prepared a substantial team of very fast Falcon saloons, and had bought the services of such distinguished racing drivers as Jo Schlesser, Henri Greder, and Graham Hill. In the face of all these, and the ever present menace of expert Erik Carlsson in a SAAB, in the face of unexpectedly dry weather in the closing stages which gave no real advantage to front-drive cars, Hopkirk's Mini won outright, and was so well supported by Aaltonen and Makinen that the Minis again took home the team prize. Suspicions founded by the original 850 Mini and made stronger by the Mini Cooper were confirmed by the Cooper S: it was a giant-killer.

Within a couple of months there were two more versions, as had been envisaged. One was a 970cc version, aimed at the 1-litre class of the European Saloon Car racing championship (duly won by Warwick Banks), and built in quantities just enough to make it eligible. The other was the car that would soon be the definitive S, with a 1275cc engine that would fit into the 1.3-litre class for racing and for rallying as well. They did not vary much in power from the 70bhp 1071: the 970cc gave 68bhp but stayed smooth and durable at very high sustained speeds, while the 1275cc gave 75 but with a wealth of low-speed torque and flexibility.

Left Hopkirk clips the apex of the corner at *le Tabac*

Mini Cooper—winner of the 1964 Monte Carlo Rally

Your BMC car may never have to take the pounding of an international rally
(but it's nice to know that it could)

What a riotous career, what fabulous successes, what admiration and delight and sheer wonder, came the way of these cars! Motoring sport was flourishing in Britain as never before: mere club events enjoyed crowds of 30,000 at winter meetings, attendance swelling to huge numbers throughout every summer weekend. More and more circuits were opened all over the country; more and more events were oversubscribed; more and more people based their choices of road cars on the extent to which racing versions appeared persuasive. Mini Coopers in every imaginable size and state ran against big cars, against each other, against the clock, sometimes against all reason: in one event where particularly wild driving resulted from the equality of so many of the Minis, the Mallory Park stewards called the entire field in for a severe reprimand.

All over Europe, people went driving with similar exuberance. In a 1965 that was to prove exceptional, Timo Makinen started with an incredibly virtuosic drive through nearly impossible blizzard conditions to win the Monte Carlo Rally, his 1275 S the only car to arrive at the principality unpenalized. The works Minis also won the Circuit of Ireland, the Geneva, the Czechoslovak, the Polish, the Finnish 1,000 Lakes, the Three Cities and the RAC rallies. That string of successes might have seemed the result of highly professional management; but private owners took the Basco-Navarrais, the Flowers and Perfumes, the Lorraine, the Austrian Gold Cup, the Bodensee, the Saragossa, the Armagnac and the Portuguese rallies, which suggested that the sheer merit of the Mini played no little part in the proceedings. In a year that saw the last outings of the big Austin-Healeys, which had once been the prime BMC entries in major rallies, the Mini won a total of 17 international rallies, with some 116 major awards in rallies and races of international status. The first three places in the rally championship for drivers went to Mini drivers Rauno Aaltonen, Tony Ambrose and Timo Makinen; it was the first time that the championship had been won with a British car.

Right Monte Carlo Rally, 1965
Top left RAC Rally, 1965
Bottom left 1000 Lakes Rally, 1965

Above Makinen and Easter on their way to Monte Carlo

The following year, 1966, opened with the most notorious Monte Carlo Rally in the long history of the event. The French had been making it clear that they did not intend to let the Mini take the laurels for a third time running; that they were not going to be hoodwinked by cars that did not meet the rules; that indeed they expected a French victory. They changed the rules to assist their purposes; they challenged the closeness of the 1275 S to the production car (only to find to their dismay that there had indeed been more

than 5,000 examples made and sold); and after the BMC Minis finished in first, second and third places overall, they went to unprecedented extremes during the following technical inspections to try to prove that the cars infringed the rules. Every objection was clearly countered, as they stripped each car down for the measurement and verification of the most trivial components. When every mechanical possibility had been exhausted, they turned to the electrics, and in final triumph they declared the Minis

Right RAC Rally, 1966
Below Monte Carlo
Rally, 1966

illegal because the headlamps contained single-filament bulbs, requiring the auxiliary lamps to provide the dipped beams. This was the time when quartz halogen lamps were just coming into use, when the majority of British competitors were using them, while the French were trying to outlaw the things because they wished to retain their long-established rules demanding yellow headlamp beams, with which the light issuing from a halogen lamp was incompatible. Conveniently, Citroën, who had been observed making changes to their lighting systems just before the end of the event, stepped up to take the winning slot perforce vacated by Makinen's winning Mini.

When all the shouts and insults, the barrage of injured French innocence and noisome French newspapers, had died away, what was left? A once distinguished event that had lost its reputation and credibility, and a car that enjoyed almost worldwide sympathy for having been robbed of its rightful recognition. The enormous publicity probably did the Mini more good than most of its unchallenged successes. And when, in 1967, the Minis came back and won, convincingly, again (the victor this time was Aaltonen, with Hopkirk and Makinen agreeing that it was 'his turn anyway'), BMC enjoyed their revenge.

It was in fact another pretty good year for Minis, officially and privately, with successes galore, as far afield as New Zealand. It looked likely, though, that it would be the last such; and so it proved. Rallies were getting tougher, and within the camp it was known that the mechanics sometimes had to work miracles to bring the now ageing Minis to the finish of an event. At the same time – and especially in racing – regulations were growing more liberal in the effort to make speeds higher and thus attract more spectators: the possibilities this trend opened for larger and more conventional cars could not be realized by the Mini, the design and layout of which did not allow it to profit from the fancy suspensions, engines and transmissions now being adopted by their rivals.

Above left Makinen and Easter
Above Aaltonen and Liddon
Right Hopkirk and Crellin

Top right And it was the Aaltonen/Liddon car which beat the others to win the 1967 Monte Carlo Rally

Left Monte Carlo Rally,
1968
Below Will Laurence
leads the pack at
Lydden, 1968
Below left The Rhodes
racer makes even an
Escort look big: Brands
Hatch, 1968

Nor would it remain long relevant. In May 1968, BMC was taken over by Leyland; the new boss of what was to be known as British Leyland, Sir Donald (later Lord) Stokes, lost no time in booting out every influential BMC individual (notably Issigonis) and replacing him with a Leyland crony. He particularly turned down his thumb on all associations with Cooper: the Minis bearing that honourable name were finished. Turner and the drivers drifted away; within two years, the competitions department was completely closed.

The Mini, however, refused to go away. The new versions being sold by BLMC might now be taken up by the modest sort of customer whom Issigonis had originally had in mind; but the youth and talent of Britain had been fired and inspired by the spectacular behaviour of the competition Minis, had been more than anxious to get to grips with the new driving techniques associated with them, and persevered with them wherever and whenever it was possible – if not on the track, then on the open road, or down a country lane, or in a reasonably deserted car park.

There had in fact emerged three distinct styles of cornering the Mini, beyond the classical slow-in, fast-out and neat technique for which the car seemed not particularly suited. The oldest, but by no means to be dismissed, made use of the handbrake, applied briefly but firmly either on the approach to or at the apex of a corner. Combined with a twitch of the steering wheel, this caused the rear wheels of the Mini to lock momentarily and thus diminish their grip, sliding outward to put the car more or less sideways, while the front wheels, with the driver's foot still

Left Henry Liddon

hard down on the accelerator, were kept pointing in the requisite direction and used the engine's power to pull the car in the same direction. The use of the handbrake to assist or initiate a turn was an ancient idea, and could be traced to the earliest days of high-performance driving, long before its alleged invention as the 'bootleg' turn by American hooch-runners during the Prohibition; but it had been developed to a very high degree by the driving-test experts of Ireland, where the most popular form of competition in the 1950s had involved closing off crossroads out in the country and then performing a series of intricate manoeuvres, forward and backward and not infrequently sideways, into and out of 'garages' marked out with paint or cones.

The handbrake turn was a fine and quick way of turning a car round in the road, pretty well in its own length, without recourse to reverse gear, without even stopping. Artistically performed, it was a treat to watch, and never more so than when a neat little Mini was demonstrating it. It was displayed on one of those occasions in the 1960s when BMC laid on a private test day for journalists to try their full range of cars on some suitable airfield circuit. A Mini Cooper had its tyres pumped up hard, a stretch of tarmac was well watered (the two precautions were necessary to simulate a slippery surface), and then studious, smartly dressed Mr Aaltonen climbed aboard, with Issigonis as passenger to see how it was done.

Along the track the Mini came flying, and when it hit the water Aaltonen spun the car smartly through 180 degrees, continuing backward along the same course for a while before again tweaking the car through 180 degrees and continuing flat out along the original course and still in the original direction. It was very impressive, and it was heartwarming then to see Issigonis take the wheel and do the same thing.

Left Rauno Aaltonen

When Aaltonen and Makinen came to the BMC team, they introduced (and Hopkirk quickly learnt and perfected) a technique developed by Scandinavian drivers during the rallying career of the original SAAB, which had front-wheel drive and a freewheel transmission that made clutchless gearshifts easy. Here the driver did not touch the handbrake but instead kicked hard at the brake pedal with his left foot, while keeping his right foot firmly planted on the accelerator pedal. The effect was that the engine overcame and negated the front brakes, those at the rear twitching the car sideways as it went into the corner, pointing it in toward the exit, while

the combination of tractive effort and well-aimed steering served to haul the Mini in the desired direction. It was a neater and more subtle method than the handbrake turn, because the attack on the brake pedal might be graduated from momentary to prolonged; it was better at getting a driver out of trouble should he enter a corner too fast; but it was difficult and time-consuming to learn. Again, it was a method that required front-wheel drive, but was not limited to the Mini although nothing did it so well – especially the 1275 S, so replete in torque that gearshifts were less likely to prove necessary in the course of the manoeuvre.

Something similar, modified only in the use of racing tyres and in having the car set up to be basically neutral in its steering responses rather than understeering as a conventional Mini would, was the method chosen by a very few racing drivers – most spectacularly and notoriously John Rhodes – who found it expedient to put the Mini completely sideways on the approach to a bend (curves were less acute on racing circuits than on rallying tracks) and then use the engine's power to pull the car along the desired trajectory, gradually straightening up as it emerged from the corner. Using necessarily hard-compound tyres (which still did not last very long!) and spending much of the time in a corner generating clouds of smoke from the spinning and scorching inside front wheel, Rhodes not only saved the brakes of the Mini from abuse but also made it difficult for any rival to overtake him on the way into a corner.

In the earlier days when Mini brakes were conspicuously weak, many drivers avoided touching them at all, but twitched the wheel briefly on the approach to the corner while momentarily releasing the accelerator. As soon as the car had developed a sideways attitude, which it would do with great alacrity, the engine would be summoned to full urge again, and the Mini would carve a great swathe through the corner before progressively straightening while accelerating away. This technique did not depend on front-wheel drive; indeed it resembled a method often used by the great GP driver Tazio Nuvolari when driving classical front-engined rear-drive racing cars in the 1930s. He said that using the brakes only made the car go more slowly! Instead, he wore his tyres to a frazzle, but it was often the better course to adopt in cars whose brakes were in any case very poor.

Below Twisting Rhodes, as on page 101

Whichever the method adopted for putting the Mini sideways, the crowds loved to watch it, and were joyously uncritical of the effect, which was actually to make the Mini faster than its rivals into a corner but slower out of it. What the Man in the Grandstands appreciated, when he left the circuit in his Mini and became once again the Man in the Street, was the basic virtue of the car in responding to modulation of the throttle pedal while cornering. Fundamentally the production Mini was a car that understeered, so that when cornering hard it would tend to run wide and ultimately steer itself off at a tangent to the intended cornering line. If in these circumstances the accelerator pedal were partially or wholly released, the change in the stresses to which the front tyres were subjected would allow them to generate more cornering power than before, so that the car would tighten its line and recover its course. Overdone, this technique would cause the car to spin, as racing driver Christabel Carlisle observed when a tyro: 'I had heard the lads in the bar say that when you lifted off the tail came round, and when I tried it I discovered what they meant!' However, a little practised skill in using the throttle pedal would allow the car to be sensitively steered by it, allowing its naturally high cornering abilities to be exploited to their utmost.

Even today, bar-room talk among drivers continues to refer to liftoff oversteer, although today it is at least as likely to apply to some tail-happy Porsche as to some nose-heavy front-drive car; but it was the Mini that made us all aware of the phenomenon, taught us how to control and exploit it, and sent us merrily on our hectic ways. Things have not changed in principle, only in degree: today's tyres are broader and grippier, and the transition from understeer to neutral- or oversteer may be gentler, but on the other hand there is often more tractive effort available from today's engines than from the older ones, so the throttle pedal can still play its vital and fascinating part.

Meanwhile, the Mini, which would never go away altogether, has continued its racing career, still the vehicle for many a modestly endowed but joyously enthusiastic young driver. It has abandoned the rallying scene, as far as events of major importance are concerned, but it is still a car ready to go anywhere and attempt anything. For a while it starred (and played most of the crowd roles as well) in rallycross, a quick and remarkably dirty negotiation of a serpentine and muddy track in full view of the television cameras which made millions aware of what could be done – and of what might be done to you if you were not watchful!

Even on the public highway, nobody was safe from the ravages of the cocky little Mini in the hands of an equally exuberant driver. Many a respectable person, going respectably in a respectable car, was carved up – perhaps mercilessly, perhaps in good humour – by a Mini that bore in its rear window a sticker announcing that YOU HAVE BEEN MINI'D!

Very often, that Mini would have been modified. Sometimes it went to one of the known tuning shops; sometimes the work was done by the owner, buying 'bolt-on goodies' that were widely available. Sometimes, the best work was done inside the cabin, where the original sit-up-and-beg driving position did no good either to control or to comfort. Issigonis joked about it, as was his style: he said that it was a deliberate artifice to ensure that the driver was kept alert. The truth was that it was part of his way of making space in the cabin so that the original Mini could be a genuine four-seater.

Above Broadspeed
Cooper S

Left opposite
Autocross makes Mini
mucky
Left bottom Jonathan
Buncombe at Mallory
Park, 1972

For the young and sportive, there was seldom a serious need for four seats; a special proprietary seat, one of several available from specialist manufacturers, would be installed for the driver, allowing him to recline somewhat and incidentally creating the extra headroom needed for wearing a helmet when driving in official competitions. A cheap and simple spacer allowed the steering column to be raked downward and backward, with perhaps a fancy wood-rimmed or leather-bound steering wheel of reduced diameter on the end of it. Thus comfortably ensconced and duly belted in (which was another detail Issigonis omitted from the original car, seat harness being extremely rare in the 1950s), the driver now found that he could not reach the rocker switches somewhere beyond his knees, so extenders became another regular fashion feature. So did a tachometer – perversely, not even the raciest Cooper S ever had one as standard!

Top left 1998 Mini Cooper LE meets 1960s Mini Cooper racer
Left The Interior of the 1998 Mini – more sumptuous than those of its 1960s predecessors

It was all part of the fun, and it remained fun (most of it harmless) even if the car never ventured near any kind of race, sprint or rally. Better than being merely harmless, better for speed and safety alike, was the popular endorsement of the latest and most modern tyres and wheels. By 1965 the limitations of the original ten-inch wheels and slender bias-ply tyres were being too readily reached even in ordinary road driving, while in racing the special tyres that had to be created for the Mini had to endure agonies of high temperature – driven by the likes of Rhodes, racing tyres reached tread temperatures as high as 130°C, at a time when even Formula One racing tyres were not expected to cope with more than 100°C. The answer was a larger-diameter wheel (the chosen figure was twelve inches) with a wider rim, shod with a wider tyre of lower profile: with less flexure to generate internal heat, with a larger contact patch to improve traction, and with a relatively shallower sidewall which enhanced steering response, such a tyre had everything to commend it and was indeed the salvation of the high-performance Mini.

Left A Mini Cooper S rally car at Goodwood, 1994

It was during the 1960s that Britain, Germany and Italy were learning slowly to adopt the radial-ply tyres that (although originally a British invention dating back to 1913) had become predominant in France. For the French motorist, Michelin being only indigenous tyre manufacturer pursuing the matter seriously, the choice was that of Mr Hobson; in the other countries, a variety of tyremakers vied with each other to produce new 'radials' that were not too dependent on Michelin patents and were with any luck more suited to local conditions. Not until 1969, when Pirelli invented the nylon 'bandage' (a cleverly tensioned belt of nylon threads running parallel to the tread and retaining the underlying steel-cord belt to prevent it from expanding or distorting), did the radial-ply tyre really come into its own.

Now the tyre could be made truly wide and low in profile, the sidewalls truly shallow, the better to realize the conceptual advantages of radial-ply construction. In the 1970s we saw the beginnings of a trend towards bigger wheels with broader, shallower tyres, at first on costly high-performance cars and gradually on cheaper and more commonplace machines, a trend that continues today, when the post-1996 Mini Cooper can be ordered with light-alloy wheels 13 inches in diameter, with rims no less than 6 inches wide to give proper support to tyres 175mm wide and only 50% of that in sidewall height.

Yes, the Mini Cooper. Stokes killed it; but the Cooper, like the Mini in general, refuses to go away. It was revived in 1990, when it proved that the public (not only in Britain, nor less as far afield as Japan) retained fond memories of it as a car that conveyed inimitable distinction. No longer the 100mph personal vibrator that tuned S versions had been in the decade when personal vibrators first went on open sale, the Cooper is still a lively and agile car, a pert statement of attitude and intent. Perhaps it is still a sports car (it does at least have a tachometer); beyond doubt it is a sight for sore eyes.

'John Cooper paid me to drive – but he didn't have to.'

John Rhodes

'Great for cheering yourself up, but only with a brilliant sound system to pump out 60s singles and drown the A-series racket.'

MARK HUGHES

international
impudent
patriotic
Film idol

In a farming district in Italy, back in 1921, a boy was born and eight days later was named Ivo Livi. He was, as the name suggests, the son of Jewish parents, and when the Fascist regime took control of the country a year later they judged it prudent to leave. At the age of two, little Ivo found himself with them in Marseille. At the age of eighteen, he found himself popular as a music-hall singer. At the age of twenty-four he found himself the protégé of the famous *chanteuse* Edith Piaf, appearing in a film called *Etoile Sans Lumière*, and using the stage name Yves Montand. To many filmgoers he seemed the epitome of worldly Gallic charm; but he soared to international stardom in 1953 with a tough role in the Jean Renoir classic *La Salaire de la Peur*.

It was a tough film by the standards of those days, when profuse violence was not yet the standard padding for almost everything on the screen. It had a truly cliffhanging ending: having successfully transported a load of nitro-glycerine across difficult country in Central America (never mind why), he was driving back exultant, swinging the truck gleefully from side to side ... until it slid out of his control, ending balanced precariously on the edge of a precipice with his reward in the back, over the ravine, and with himself a desperately counterpoised balance-weight in the cab. With his slightest move, the truck threatened to topple over the edge ...

Above and far left
British hooligans in Italy

143

The Italian

Sixteen years later, Michael Caine and a crew of uproariously rejoicing British crooks are in a motor coach that has been converted as a transporter, haring over a pass in the Italian Alps with their booty of bullion in baskets in the back. The driver, exultant, is swinging the transporter gleefully from side to side ...

until it slides out of his control, ending balanced precariously on the edge of a precipice with the bullion right at the back, over the ravine, and with all the crew desperately still as balance-weights at the forward end. When any of them makes a move, the transporter threatens to topple over the edge.

Above Minis keeping bad company

J

These patriotically coloured cars serve as the getaway vehicles for the British crooks after their meticulously planned and audaciously executed robbery of a consignment of gold bullion in Torino. The city's traffic, chaotic at the best of times, has been cleverly paralyzed: the only way out of the town is an intricate convolution of backlanes, stairways, roofs and a car park, sewers and a weir. The Italian police in their Italian cars are mercilessly humiliated. Some beautiful Nervi architecture and Fiat's stunning Mirafiore factory lend their contours to the scenery of the chase, and the Minis take every opportunity to show off their formidable repertoire of tricks, including handbrake turns and reverse flicks.

This is the end of *The Italian Job*. It is exciting stuff, but it is comedy rather than intense drama. As well as Michael Caine, the cast includes Noel Coward, Fred Emney, Benny Hill, a generous measure of decorative young ladies, a Lamborghini Miura, sundry Aston Martins and E-type Jaguars, Fiat Dino Coupés, Alfa Romeo police cars and a monstrous Caterpillar mobile shovel; but the real stars are a red Mini Cooper S, a white Mini Cooper S, and a blue Mini Cooper S.

Above and right
It goes down stairs well too

The whole escapade is done in an excess of exuberance. When hurtling through the circular-section sewer tunnels, the Minis flick from side to side, first up one wall and then up the other. In the making of this shot, one or two Minis were written off in an attempt to perform a full barrel roll; others were sacrificed while perfecting similarly high-spirited stunts. The last part of the film is nothing more than a celebration of the speed, the controllability, the grip and agility, the impudence and the utter Britishness, of the Mini-Cooper S. Such a shame, when the credits rolled, to see that the team of stunt drivers employed was not a bunch of mad young English racing drivers but the French and sternly professional Equipe Rémy Julienne.

It was no less a shame to see how somebody had duped Fiat into lending their assistance, and obtaining the collaboration of the Torino authorities, for the making of the film. Torino is Fiat's home city – some would go further and declare it to be Fiat's city – and the film could not have been made without massive co-operation from its factories, its shops, its police, its people. More was asked than mere accommodation: three beautiful Fiat Dino Bertone Coupés were destroyed in the filming of one brief scene, and the cost to Fiat of closing at least one factory and arranging other facilities must have been enormous. In return for all this, they and all their cars and all that they stood for were ridiculed.

The Minis apart, the British contingent did not show up in a much better light, most of them appearing to non-British audiences to be ill-mannered and perfidious felons bereft of all civilizing principles. In retrospect, the only people to be portrayed in the film as punctilious, elegant, disciplined, cultivated, and discreet in the exercise of their considerable power, were the Mafia.

Perhaps that explains why it is not easy to discover who did the vital negotiating before *The Italian Job*, a film of enormous and lasting commercial success and similarly enduring popularity and influence, was made?

Left They that…
occupy their business
in great waters

Above Ballistic trajectory
Below Balletic agility

number

For films less dominated by a car or cars, such negotiations are commonly the work of the car manufacturer's publicity department, either the advertising agency or the public relations department – if not, in some rare display of unison, both. Publicists know well enough that the mere exposure of the firm's product in a film, even a film of fairly humdrum calibre, will make a favourable impression on the multitudes who will view it. The film-maker seldom has to ask, never expects to pay. The car maker will furnish a car for filming, one or two more for rehearsals, perhaps others for shooting in remote locations; there may also be cars for the leading actors and actresses, for the director, for the producer, for the chief cameraman. The car maker will not expect to see any of these cars ever again. Were they to be returned, they would be in disgraceful condition, having been used and abused by every individual surrounding the making of the film – and that is a lot of people. The publicity, according to the publicists, is worth it.

There are times when the film-makers have their own particular views on the suitability of a car for the part it has to play. It seemed appropriate – and it certainly generated enormous publicity – that James Bond should be served by a deviously armed Aston Martin. If when we watched the film it seemed curious that this magnificent race-bred supercar could not get away from the ordinary Mercedes-Benz saloon being driven in pursuit by the Baddies, we took the most forgiving view, assuming that it was because of the needs of the plot. We all still applauded the Aston Martin; some of us may even have gone out and bought one.

Right opposite
The Mini Moke taxi,
as used in the 60s TV
series, *The Prisoner*
Left Peter Sellers and
basket case

When Peter Sellers was acting the male lead, opposite Elke Sommer, in *A Shot in the Dark*, it seemed to him that the car he drove in the film had to be the car that he drove on the road. The film was one in a series presenting Sellers as Inspector Clouseau, and, although he insisted that he was personally a blank from which each character could be formed, his large and admiring public already tended to identify Sellers and Clouseau – in which case the Clouseau car should be recognizably the Sellers car.

The car that Sellers drove on the road was a Mini, but one that was very special indeed, the one that had been revised, retrimmed, refitted, refined, replated, repolished and re-formed by Hooper & Co of St James's, London, coach builders to the carriage trade. For Hooper, slightly suspicious of cars and people that might not unquestioningly be esteemed of carriage-trade quality, once was enough: they declined to repeat the exercise. Instead, the livelier and younger (and, if anything, cheaper) Harold Radford firm, pleased to build shooting brakes on Bentleys but content to put soft tops on Volvos if such was the customer's modest ambition, was avid to take up the cause of the luxury Mini and positively hungry for the publicity that the film should yield.

Wicker panelling and all, Radford aped the Hooper Mini – but the car for the film had a Downton engine, the power of which more than compensated for the extra weight and drag of the luxury trimmings. For occasional scenes filmed on location in France, for which it would have been too costly to ship the star car back and forth (most of *A Shot in the Dark* was shot under the lights of the Pinewood Studios in England), a French 850 Mini with a similar external paint job was substituted, and there are to this day people who derive some excitement from spotting the appearances of this car in the film. There are even suggestions that there were three cars, and that Sellers' own original Hooper was used in some scenes.

The Mini Moke was well cast in its starring role in the 1967 cult TV series *The Prisoner*. Created by actor-director Patrick McGoohan, who played the title role, the series continues to inspire a wealth of interpretations, from a defence of the individual in a totalitarian society to a psychedelic trip. All that we ever know about the Prisoner is that he is unable to leave the Village where he is held, that he is known as number 6 and that he used to be a spy. The only form of transport in the Village is the Moke taxi service, but, like the Prisoner, the individualistic little cars are unable to leave the confines of the town. The series was partly filmed in Sir Clough Williams-Ellis's picturesque village of Portmeirion, where every available garage was filled with a Moke for weeks on end. The Moke still enjoys immense popularity in Portmeirion.

A certain television series which prolonged the practices of the film industry for months, and eventually years, on end was *The Avengers*, which seemed to have something to do with hot-blooded and cool-minded Brits privily taking arms against a motley sea of Dastardly Foreigners seeking to subvert all that was good and secure and – well, British. Auxiliary to the keen eye and steady hand of the hero, John Steed, played by Patrick Macnee were the keen hands (and feet!) and roving eyes of Honor Blackman, than whom few could be better qualified to demonstrate the properties of a miniskirt. Subservient to both of these characters, but not at all averse to stealing the scene when there was an opportunity to show off all that was British and therefore best, was often a Mini. With its weight carried low, with its wide stance and stumpy tail and stocky body, its squat nose and undershot chin and inbred disinclination to let go, there was quite an air of the bulldog about it.

On other occasions, it was just a dog. The dash down to Devon for the first wedding featured in *Four Weddings and A Funeral* was in a Mini that had doubtless seen better days. The poor thing may have been lamentable, may even have been deplorable, but the honest basic Mini cannot be embarrassed. Many an ordinary Mini, standing around or driving around in many a film and perhaps noticed only subliminally by the unsuspectingly susceptible viewer, has been a perfectly ordinary Mini.

Left The Avengers: John Steed (Patrick Macnee), Emma Peel (Diana Rigg) and a Mini Moke

Below Rowan Atkinson and a Mini in the TV Series, *Mr Bean*

Nevertheless, people in show business need to show themselves off as successful. Should they have populist consciences or other left-wing tendencies, they may find it tactful to be *modestly* successful. If it accordingly suits the image of some such celebrity (and there have been many such) to be seen with a Mini, it had better be a lavishly decorated Mini. If one really wishes to be seen, there can logically be no substitute for a Mini Moke; but if one does not wish to be seen as a drowned rat, it had better be a fancy-looking saloon Mini. Show-business celebrities galore made some sort of point of having one, and in some cases may even have paid for it, though public appearance with such people is, like a film appearance, recognized by publicists as being a potentially profitable investment. If the celebrity did pay, the cost was doubtless set against taxable income as a business expense.

Below A typically British scene with sheep, stone walls and a Mini, in *Three Men and a Little Lady*, 1990

Heads of State presumably are not faced with such problems. When the state is a republic, it is rare for its leader to display himself in anything so populist as a Mini; crowned heads, happy, if not even anxious, to identify themselves with their people, are a different matter. Prince Rainier of Monaco was very keen on motor racing (he took the trouble to have his distinguished subject Louis Chiron, one of the cleverest racing drivers of his time, teach him the arts of driving quickly, and was fond of driving cars in which those arts could be practised), but his consort Princess Grace chose a Mini. So did King Constantine of Greece, whose car was later acquired by the actor Lawrence Harvey: he commissioned Wood &

Above The Italian Job
special edition of 1992

Pickett to revamp the upper rear quarters, turning the Mini into a rather fetching little opera coupé complete with dummy hood irons and a tiny elliptical rear window. It was still not a true *de ville* body, any more than the original Radford Mini de Ville had a true *de ville* body, the essence of which is that the front seats where the chauffeur operates are open to the weather while the rear quarters are enclosed and accorded decent privacy. Very few people knew that; even fewer know it today; fewer still care.

There can be, after all, little concern with reality for people in a business that turns entirely on appearances. The makers of the Mini did not even bother, when they offered their 1992 special edition named The Italian Job, with making the car look authentic: all manner of details were different from those of the cars in the original film, and one could even have the special edition painted in green. Publicity makes whatever noise it thinks loudest, rather than worrying about purity of tone.

ROVER

The Italian Job, the finest advertisement the Mini ever had, inspired more than a mere special edition. In 1990 began an annual series of celebration runs from England to Italy and back, requiring entrants to drive their Minis in unpredictable early-winter weather across Switzerland and the Stelvio Pass into Italy, to undertake a regularity run and an autotest and a sprint or two, to navigate themselves through a series of vineyards, collecting bottles of Italian wine which were not to be opened until they were in England. Further obligations were a tour of the BMW museum in München, a visit to the Nurburgring racing circuit (where a lap of the historic Nordschleife was a DM14 option) and a visit to one of the SOS Children's Villages. In fact, the whole exercise is a charitable one, raising money for the SOS Children's Villages in Italy and the NSPCC (National Society for the Prevention of Cruelty to Children) in Britain. There can be a hundred Minis taking part, and *still* they generate publicity.

It's pure sporting chic.
...still generating publicity

'Among other attributes, it enabled people to steer

around accidents instead of becoming involved in them.'

'STEADY' BARKER journalist

refurbished
reconsidered
refined
Freak

'All that moveth doth in Change delight,' according to Spenser. Literary academics may have missed a chance to vindicate him because, if the metamorphoses of the Mini are evidence, it rather looks as though dear old Edmund S was right, even though he was 400 years premature.

Of all the things that move, save only the works of the dog breeders and skirt makers of this world, can anything have been so shortened, lengthened, raised, lowered, slimmed, fattened, filleted, gutted, rejigged, refurbished, repainted, refined, reconsidered – yet never replaced – as the Mini?

Left Valerie Jane
pulls Piccadilly eyes
over her wool

Left The Coachbuilt
Mini Limo

To alter the Mini, to change anything and everything except its identity as a Mini, has become a means of livelihood for many a business, a way of life for many an enthusiast. Unlike the modifications made to dogs and possibly to skirts, it is seldom the result of any major dissatisfaction with the characteristics of the breed. Such people as truly dislike the Mini invariably *change it* for something else, and sooner or later after the exchange learn either to regret that move, or to go to extremes in justifying it; and there are also some people who never learn.

No, it is not dissatisfaction that lies at the bottom of this sea of change. It may be curiosity or whimsy, vanity or vainglory, meddling or meta–physics, that prompts someone to modify a Mini to make it their own, to make it like no other, even to make it as remote as possible from the reality of a Mini while yet contriving to keep it a Mini. Any or many of these it may be; but almost invariably an overwhelming sense of fun is involved.

Below Interior features of the Mini Limo include Wilton carpets and a special stereo system developed by Rover Engineering and Alpine

Below The Coachbuilt Mini Limo is the most expensive and luxurious Mini ever

Above The circus comes to Brands Hatch

MIN-URE HEAP

Above The lengths
some people will go to

Hobbyists are strange folk. Psychologists tend to
see hobbyists as mildly obsessional personalities.
Something or other – music or art if the patient
be fortunate; tiddlywinks or train timetables if not
– lays fast hold on the hobbyist and he or she
retreats to a lifetime study of it, seeking out like-
minded unfortunates in some club or association.

If the associative link with his or her fellows is the
Mini, then the hobbyist feels eligible for their
society by having a Mini. They seek to be a
recognized member, so they do whatever may be
necessary to make theirs a distinctive Mini. If
they hope for rank and power in that society, they
do whatever makes theirs a superior Mini, very
often by changing so much of it that the
inescapable essential identity of the Mini stands
out by being isolated.

They begin to idolize the Mini, to see it as the
fountain of all good, to be blind to its deficiencies.
It becomes something deserving all their leisure
time and energy all their disposable money, all
their partisan persuasiveness. It monopolizes,
hypnotizes, and seems more and more to deserve
all the things that they can do for it or to it.

What those things are depends on time and
capability. The skills he or she is able to deploy
may be those cultivated in their trade or acquired
during their upbringing: they may be a proficient
mechanic, for example, or may have learnt to
paint. The way in which the chosen skill is
applied will probably be a function of their times,
and of the fashions that they support. Thus in the
1960s, when the reputation of the Mini as a
formidable racing or rallying machine reached its
zenith, the mechanics might modify their own
cars to echo the practices of the paddock. The
painters might prefer to adopt the contemporary
usages of pop art and adorn their cars with
portraits, flames, scrolls and sunsets or tins of
soup. *This* Mini has widened wheel-arches and
half a dozen headlamps, because that is how the
works cars rallied. *That* Mini is covered in old,
predecimalization English pennies, because the
Beatles had sung 'Penny Lane'. *This* Mini has
been lowered until its big-bore exhaust pipe
barely clears the ground. *That* Mini has been
glossed with candy-apple flaked lacquer wherever
chromium plating has been impracticable – *so*
elegant, don't you think, with the Afghan
goatskins draped over the back seat?

Below So much art on
so little a Mini

The most common craze in the first dozen years of the Mini was for high-performance conversions. Britain was peppered with little tuning shops, a few of them run by respected engineers but the majority by hopeful mechanics who imitated without understanding and frequently made things worse. Many a customer was not worried, having chosen the path of multiple carburettors and magical camshafts, of widened track and lowered stance, purely for audio-visual effect. In fact, the fatter tyres on wide-rimmed wheels almost always proved beneficial, enhancing the Mini's already notable alacrity in steering and stability in cornering, while often improving braking performance into the bargain. As for lowering the little car, bringing its centre of gravity even closer to the ground and to the roll axis, it could not fail to improve everything, so long as the car was not taken where ground clearance might be a problem.

Left Broadspeed's restored 1966 Austin Mini Cooper S 1275. Its interior is that of the classic Mk I Cooper S – Tartan red and Porcelain grey with gold brocade. This Mini now resides in Portugal and as such a fine specimen, frequently features in classic car articles on the Cooper S

Above The Speedwell Sprint

Lowering the car from the bottom was limited, by the nature of things. Lowering it from the top and from the middle became a craze independent of the racing scene where it began. Some track folk, seeing the virtue of minimizing frontal area, had lowered their roofs somewhat – and, presumably, their seats – but racer-journalist Clive Trickey proposed slicing 1.5 inches out of the windows and pillars, and another 1.5 between the floor and the waistline. The seats were lowered and reclined, the round headlamps exchanged for rectangular ones, and the result was called the Mini Sprint, rather irrelevantly, perhaps to distinguish it from the one-word Minisprint, which was a cheaper and possibly earlier rival version. Its brief popularity outlasted its usefulness, and the issue of a second series 1.25 inches shallower still did little to prolong either.

The appeal of the idea to the young and earnestly zany did in time lead to other expressions of the same idea: Scott Lloyd shaved nine inches out of a Mini; and eventually Andy Saunders – allowing or indeed encouraging the engine to poke up through the bonnet, ahead of a windscreen only six inches deep – brought the whole thing down by fourteen inches, contrived to have it accepted by the 1988 *Guinness Book of Records* as the lowest car in the world (which I doubt), and named it Claustrophobia.

Other people found the idea of a lowered Mini easier to embody if it did not have to look like a Mini. Because its mechanical essentials were mounted on sub-frames, it was an easy thing to accomplish. In 1966, Ralph Broad, proprietor of one of the really effective tuning shops trading as Broadspeed, built a new long-tailed fastback body to replace the top half of a highly tuned Mini 1275, and sold about thirty examples. Broadspeed are still very much in business today, running a highly successful outfit specializing in restoring and customizing minis for people all over the world.

Below Broadspeed's 1966 GT Coupé – more commonly known as the 'Mini Aston Martin'

Rather more thorough, Marcos in darkest Wiltshire made a whole new streamlined body of glass-reinforced plastics, bolted the Mini sub-frames into it, and thus created the Mini-Marcos. Jem Marsh, who provided half the name of the firm, was an astute racing businessman; his partner Frank Costin, who provided the other half, was a clever engineer and exceptional aerodynamicist. The result was the only British car to finish in the 1966 24 Heures du Mans, which helped its sales for quite a few years.

Other people saw that, by putting the Mini engine pack behind the driver, a sports car of minute proportions could be endowed with the dynamic character of the latest and most modern racers. From this realization was born the Cox GTM, in a shapely and compact body. With a well-tuned engine to exploit the car's light weight and quite good shape, it performed brilliantly, and business was good for many years after the 1969 introduction.

Below The Mini Marcos

An even better car did scarcely any business at all. The Unipower GT, a production sideline of a firm making forestry tractors, was a very low (41 inches), very light and most efficiently shaped rear-engined combination of body and multi-tubular steel chassis. It was very well (and, as it turned out, uneconomically) made and in my experience very satisfying to drive. In the last four years of the 1960s some 75 were made.

Even less success attended the hobby of former Lotus designer Brian Luff. He was also responsible for the Clan Crusader, a nice little Imp-engined coupé that exploited the clamshell construction that had recently been invented for a new Lotus shortly before he left the firm. His Mini-based Status was formed in the same angular and faceted fashion as those two, was always orange, and was never highly regarded. His rear-engined Minipower, an open two-seater, with suspension like that of current racing single-seaters, did decently in hill climbs but was not a convincing bargain for the open road.

Above The Mini Speedster, designed by Mini Speed, is a Mini adaption which makes use of a Mini's main structure and nose

Quite the opposite applied to the Ogle Mini. This much admired little 2+2 coupé was a product of the industrial design outfit that later created some attractive versions of the biggest Reliant cars, including a well-glazed estate for Prince Philip. Strongly backed and energetically marketed, but sternly opposed by BMC when there was a possibility of its being made in quantity by Jensen, the Ogle Mini foundered soon after David Ogle died in a road accident.

The list continues, long and wearying. The Jimini looked like a Moke. The Scamp looked something like it, but even worse. The 140 mph Landar looked like a miniature CanAm racer. The Crayford Convertible looked like a perambulator. The Biota looked like nothing on earth. There were also about eighty examples sold of a Mini rebuilt at the nose to look like a miniature Rolls-Royce: litigious Rolls-Royce were not amused, but the cynical creator of this send-up, Brian Luff again, thought it a huge joke.

Above From the Mini came Issigonis' Princess. This converted model, made to resemble a Rolls-Royce, was designed by Van Den Plas

Below An Austin Mini 850 convertible, by Crayford

Above A spare tyre for each corner

Above Stop him and buy one

There were indeed jokers galore among the ranks of the Mini-mouldbreakers. The film producer who had a Mini decapitated to make an aero-screened barchetta, Hunky Dory, designed to be davited between-decks on board his luxury yacht, was joking; otherwise, he would have called it John. The chap who put giant rear tyres on his front-drive car had to be joking. The chap who inserted four feet of bodywork amidships to create a limousine – a chap called Haynes, who laboured for more than 4,000 hours on it – probably thought it was a joke of sorts, though he exploited it commercially. So did the firm of peripatetic exhaust fitters who supported an extra-long pick-up with an extra pair of wheels under the tail. So did Gurch Samra, proprietor of the Coventry firm Car Electronics, whose long six-wheeler saloon was filled with audio apparatus of high quality and great violence, scoring 138 dB in those vicious 'sound-off' competitions that became a feature of 1990s life among the anoraks. His joke was the punning name given to the car, Extended Bass.

Some of the most extreme transformations were uncompromisingly professional publicity tools. Duckham's, the oil company, used a tubular steel frame and a Ford back axle to replace the bulk of a Mini and give it a very short wheelbase, above which soared a huge effigy of a can of Duckham's. It was no more than a mobile advertisement hoarding (in which respect it was the equal of most racing cars since about 1970), whereas the Mini Orange was more adaptable.

Right No place like home

Capespan, purveyors of Outspan oranges, ordered five specimens of this weird Mini. The basis was a spherical shell, dimpled and painted to resemble an orange, complete with a green stalk on its crown. The 1972 prototype had a hinged top half, but opening it was heavy work, and instead a door was hinged into the back, behind a wheelbase of only 48 inches. All the glass was curved, all of it but the windscreen orange-tinted; all the interior was orange coloured. That interior was also unventilated, which must have made the promotional girl inside quite glad to get out and, flaunting her big basket of fruit and her voluminous folk dress, mingle with the crowds.

Above and right

Outspan's oranges were
based on automatic
Minis

Though it was hot and sticky work for her, doubtless the bosses and the customers thought it great fun. Doubtless the men who went in for strenuous competition driving thought that fun, too, but they always went about it so seriously that we may beg leave to doubt it. Consider Nick Paddy, prime mover of a firm specializing in fancy Minis for the burgeoning market in Japan in the mid-90s. It was as much for commercial ends as for fun that he commissioned the building of a pick-up (chosen for its light weight, essential to acceleration) that would be finished to *concours* standards and would be powered by the most rabid Mini power pack that could be inserted. Impelled by a 1400cc engine of truly spectacular composition, the Paddy pick-up ran a standing-start quarter-mile in 14.78 seconds, crossing the finishing line at 94 mph, on the Santa Pod drag strip. A week later, at the celebrations for the Mini's 35th anniversary, it won the *concours d'élégance*. Shortly after that, it went to an enchanted client in Japan. Perhaps that was the point at which Mr Paddy started having fun.

Above The Electric Mini…
Top above under the bonnet

Left and below
This Broadspeed Mini Cooper S was recreated incorporating a new Mini body shell with original Mk I Cooper S components

What looked like another high-performance pick-up was undertaken to dispel boredom, it was admitted by its maker, Ray Christopher. It may not be quite the same as having fun, but it is a step in the right direction; and he cannot have failed to enjoy the process of planning this extraordinary vehicle, so aptly named The Thug. The part that makes it look like a Mini is no more than the skin, the shell of an old Countryman, cut down and scooped out until it took on the shape of a pick-up. What it covered – or, in the case of the engine and exhausts, did not deign to cover – was a full-race chassis and suspension, all of excellent pedigree, propelled by an American V8 engine so highly tuned as to give 540bhp from its 302 in³ cylinders. It is not every day that one can enjoy a strictly street-legal car capable of sprinting over a standing-start quarter-mile in a mere nine seconds, while looking from a distance like a cosmetically treated Mini. Surely, it *must* be fun!

Sadly, high performance is no longer thought respectable by those brainwashed multitudes who, having never tried it, condemn it as antisocial, inimical to ecology, hostile to the environment, and inconsistent with the principles of conservation – even though a fast car does save time, which is the most irreplaceable and invaluable commodity of all. High performance has long ceased to be a principal feature of Mini conversions. What matters now is Art.

It has been a long process, this gradual focussing on appearance. In the world at large, where only a minority of the public has much relevant engineering understanding, cars have always been sensitive to their looks, because they are assessed by their looks. The styling of the car was at its most voluptuous in France in the 1920s, its most fantasy-laden in the USA in the 40s and 50s, its most quirky in Britain in the 60s, its most aggressive in Germany in the 90s. Until thirty years ago, the majority of cars were technically similar because the basic (and nowadays seemingly crude) methods of making them made any alternative financially risky – and it was these shackles of depressing similarity that Issigonis sought to break with the Mini. For the last thirty years, during which the majority of cars have adopted the front-drive layout with transverse engine that was pioneered by the Mini, conformity has been imposed by legislation – by the safety and emissions laws that have consistently been based on assumptions of common practice that have led to a terrible convergence of technologies in the attempt to make cars better examples of the same thing, rather than allowing different things that might or might not be better. Always keep a hold on nurse, for fear of finding something worse.

Above Decoration
sometimes stumbled
over the seams

As recounted in another chapter, the photographer became the new popular communicator. Appearances counted for everything. Stills in the press, movies on the screen, became the means whereby people judged things. Never mind what lay beneath the skin: how seductive, how conventional, how outrageous, how acceptable, the thing looked in the light of the studio (and eventually, though even that seemed less important, in the light of day) was all that mattered.

Left It could simply be commercial

There was another influence at work in this increasing focus on appearance – one almost exactly contemporary with the Mini. Television, the aptly named gogglebox, took hold. In 1960, two out of three British households had a set; by 1975, nine out of ten; today, there are more sets than households. In 1969 a quarter of all spare time was spent watching it. People became accustomed to visual presentation of anything and everything, became unfamiliar with reading. The press, terrified of being abandoned, followed suit: more and more space was devoted to pictures; technology was summoned to make coloured pictures economically feasible. Soon it would be unthinkable to devote so much as a two-page spread entirely to print, without breaking it up with pictures and other graphic entertainment for the eyes.

Right or just plain juvenile!

Above Up the creek with 4 paddles – from the sublime to the ridiculous

Modification of the Mini took on a new look. The production car, after being remarkable for its novelty and ability in its first decade, had settled down into its originally intended use as a convenient and practical vehicle for the everyday use of the modestly endowed and economically minded. Commuter, shopping car, occasional tourer – it had lost its cheekiness and some of its charm. It no longer had any enemies; but it no longer cut any ice. Only as it entered its third decade did the realization dawn that here was a car of such character that it had defied the death that comes to most cars when fashion ceases to support them. Nowhere did that realisation strike so hard as in those two acutely fashion-conscious countries, Germany and Japan.

The most superficial assessment of the Mini's suitability for Japan might recognize that the narrow streets, the crowded cities, the choked traffic, all made a car as small as the Mini (actually shorter than some of the microcars that the Japanese made for a special low-tax category of their own) eminently suitable. Add the daily difficulties of finding somewhere to park, and the high cost of residential parking (in Tokyo it is related to the size of the car, and if you have no space for it within your own domain you are not allowed even to own a car, let alone to leave it in the street), and the Mini makes even more sense. Take into account the relatively small stature of most of the population, and the literal or metaphorical shortcomings of the Mini cease to matter.

Yet there is more to Japan, and to the Japanese, than that. No society has more successfully integrated history, technology, heritage, and honour into contemporary life. The most eminent of craftsmen, artists, mystics, people who do their things in ways recognized as almost immutably perfect, are distinguished as 'living legends'. The Mini, the car meant to do well what was wanted and to make no pretensions to anything else, the car that had endured when others had come and gone as evanescent as the autumn leaves or the daily papers, the car respected for its age in a society fascinated by what is new, has been accorded similar status. One third of Mini production now goes to Japan.

Ninety per cent of those Minis are then modified in some way. It is the essence of the Mini that is recognized as defying change, not the dull detail. Light tuning, employing simple 'bolt-on goodies' (the term, used with a measure of contempt by the English who originated it, grew up with the early Mini) is commonplace. Fancy wheels and tyres are important: Pirelli had to make a special version of their classic low-profile P7 tyre just for the twelve-inch wheels of Japanese Minis. Really serious performance enhancement has its place: the fastest racing Mini in the world, ever, is probably a black carbon-fibre bat boasting a lot of original Mini parts and 180bhp, and made in Japan. Most amazing, however, is the Japanese addiction to retro-styling.

Here are history and heritage given honour. One cannot be certain about the importance of those door pockets – not without knowing what the Japanese drink in lieu of a Dry Martini Cocktail – but there is a lively trade in original tail-lights, bumpers, and radiator grilles. External door hinges, external mirrors on the wings, ten-inch wheels, drum front brakes, all these and more never-to-be-forgotten details are somehow found and incorporated. It has to look right.

Below Mini Day at the Suzuka Racing Circuit in Japan. 2,500 Minis participated in this very popular annual Mini show where attendance exceeded 40,000 people

Right This photo was taken at the Nürburg-Ring Race Circuit near Koblenz in Germany. The model on the roof is based on this Mini and was built by the car's owner

What looks right to the Germans has to look German, and should ideally look costly. It has to look positive, unequivocal. It helps to look massive; but, if the minimal size of the Mini precludes that, such masses as there are must be visually balanced: so wheel-arch extensions cannot be apologetic little strips of tin but must be large and smoothly integrated, the better to match the wide wheels and low-profile tyres that Germany (for too long notorious for turning out big, heavy and sometimes fast cars inadequately shod) now knows to be essential for good dynamic behaviour.

Neither can the German interior dare to look shabby, nor mean, nor even minimalist. Handsome wood, luxurious leather, fine wool and polished metal fill such space around the occupants as a Mini cabin offers. Lavish audio equipment fills it with Strauss or Stockhausen, or more probably some extremely loud rock. And then there is the exterior paintwork …

Paint is something that German carmakers have traditionally done well. German Mini-painters do it very well. After the conventions of national racing colours were shattered in the late 1960s by tricky Colin Chapman, head of Britain's Lotus team and hunter of sponsorship on a scale that

Grand Prix racing had never known, it was BMW who fielded a sports-racing car whose surface was an abstract painting. Porsche have caught the eye with similar high-speed canvasses several times since. At a time when the average competition car has become nothing but a billboard, sometimes with so many and so multicoloured advertisements on it that the shape and identity of the car disappear (especially in colour photographs, confound them), the surface treatment of the car as a work of art is wonderfully welcome.

So the German Mini swanking-iron is not merely filmed in exquisite expanses of expensive hand-soothed lacquer. That may be just the start, before it is then cobwebbed in delicate lines of silver lacing and interlacing at arbitrary angles over paint and glass alike. Or it may be just the background to an elaborately hand-wrought cobra in jewelled metal, coiled and poised to strike from its bonnet-top vantage where lesser cars carry badges or bruises. Even that may fail to give complete satisfaction: Stefan Imhof, whose Monster fits this description, was toying with the idea of lights in the eyes of the cobra, and a high-voltage spark (derived from the innards of a stun gun) arcing from fang to fang.

Below American-flavoured custom job from 1963

Subtlety does not have much of a place in the 1990s. There was a good deal of subtlety, however, in the original idea of a luxurious Mini, when the first such contra-diction took shape. It was the subtlety of the tragic figure acting the clown, and that clown being in turn a tragic figure. The clown, the tragic figure, and the progenitor of the idea, were all subsumed in the person of Peter Sellers.

Widely dismissed as a comedian, as one of The Goons, as one of the bright and brittle young men who in their time made Great Britain without making Britain great, Peter Sellers (if only on the evidence of *I'm All Right, Jack* and *The Waltz of the Toreadors*, not to mention other films) was an utterly brilliant actor. He modestly attributed his success to being in his private person a nullity, one so bereft of character and inbuilt characteristics that there was nothing to resist the imposition and absorption of whatever character he played. That does not sound like the confession of an anorak, of an obsessional personality. In fact, he sounds like a man whose wide-ranging interest and curiosity made it difficult to stick with any one thing for too long, and he indulged his curiosity with a great variety of cars, generally bought from or through his friend Anthony Crook, who was best known as an uncannily proficient racing driver and as the distributor of Bristol cars before he became the boss of that firm.

THERE WAS ONCE AN ACTOR called Peter Sellers who was rich and famous and who loved cars. But although he bought and sold 80 cars in 15 years he could never find the one he wanted to spend the rest of his life with. He was quite in despair until one day he decided to make his own special car.

So out he went and bought an ordinary Mini Cooper. Then, he took it to the magicians (Hooper Motor Services) and told them to wave their wands and transform this ordinary vehicle into a Sellers special. Money, he declared, was no object. 'Anything you boys can think of' he said grandly 'you have my full permission to do.'

The *electricians* fitted Bentley headlamps after modifying the wings, and put an additional flasher on the steering column. Then they put in a new heater system and wired up for electrically operated windows and a backlight demister

THE £2600 MINI

Above The wicker-flanked Sellers Cooper

In those days, away back at the beginning of the 60s but before they had really started to swing, Sellers saw that the Mini offered special promise. He was already wealthy, and the cars of the wealthy were then cars of mass and substance, of eye-filling girth and conspicuous consumption; but, under the influence of recent fuel, and other, crises, it was no longer socially acceptable to go barging around in cars so overblown and opulent, least of all in cars so thirsty. Nor indeed were they an unquestionable asset in the choked traffic and alongside the crowded kerbs of an increasingly lively London.

Sellers saw that, short of resorting to a motorcycle, the only way to get across London tolerably quickly, the only way to progress with enough improvisatory exploration of back routes to ensure decent punctuality, was by Mini. He also saw that the trimmings and trappings of the traditional luxury car need not be confined to the traditional, big, blustering braggarts. Was not the Mini recognized as a classless car, one that you could take anywhere?

He was not the first. Witty financier and diplomat Mr Nubar Gulbenkian (who was *really* wealthy) had earlier commissioned a luxury version of the standard London taxicab (alas, it was festooned with carriage lanterns, but perhaps his humour embraced Kitsch), enjoying the exploitation in London of a turning circle so tight that his conveyance could 'turn on a sixpence – whatever that is!'

Gulbenkian belonged to an earlier age; Sellers was very much a man of the 60s. He took his ideas for realisation by Hoopers, then still the most august of British custom coach builders, generally associated with their work on various Rolls-Royce chassis but not wholly averse to others. Their work was exquisite; whatever their craftsmen privately thought of the Mini, they did a beautiful job on Sellers' car. The interior was lavish, luxurious, and in what their most aristo-cratic customers would have deemed entirely acceptable taste. The exterior was not significantly changed in form, but, while all the chromium and paint was of Hooper's usual plate-glass quality, it was the decoration of the flanks in simulated wickerwork that took everybody's fancy.

Above Sellers in another Radford Mini

Again, it was not a new idea. Wicker and basketwork, long used in horse-drawn carriages, had been much favoured for the furnishing of car bodies in the early days of motoring, for it was light and springy and unexpectedly comfortable. Its memory was revived in the 1920s by some French carriage builders who were making closed bodies of outstanding chic for such noble cars as Bugatti: door panels were hand-painted on the outside to resemble wickerwork (which had also been enjoying some popularity in French drawing rooms), and the effect was much admired.

So was Peter Sellers' Mini. For all the admiration, alas, Hooper could not be persuaded to do it again. The Mini, they seemed to feel, was *infra dignitatem*. No such reservations were felt by Harold Radford, a more accessible coach builder who had been doing good work, particularly in shooting-brake or estate-car styles, on chassis of Bentley calibre. In 1963 he had a Motor Show stand displaying just such a job as Hooper had done, and demand for copies remained lively for some time, with Sellers ordering another one, with an opening tailgate.

Above This incredible bespoke Cooper S by Harold Radford was built in 1971. Created a hatch-back, it remains one of the world's best known Minis

Right The owner of this Mini loved it so much he had a highly detailed scale model built

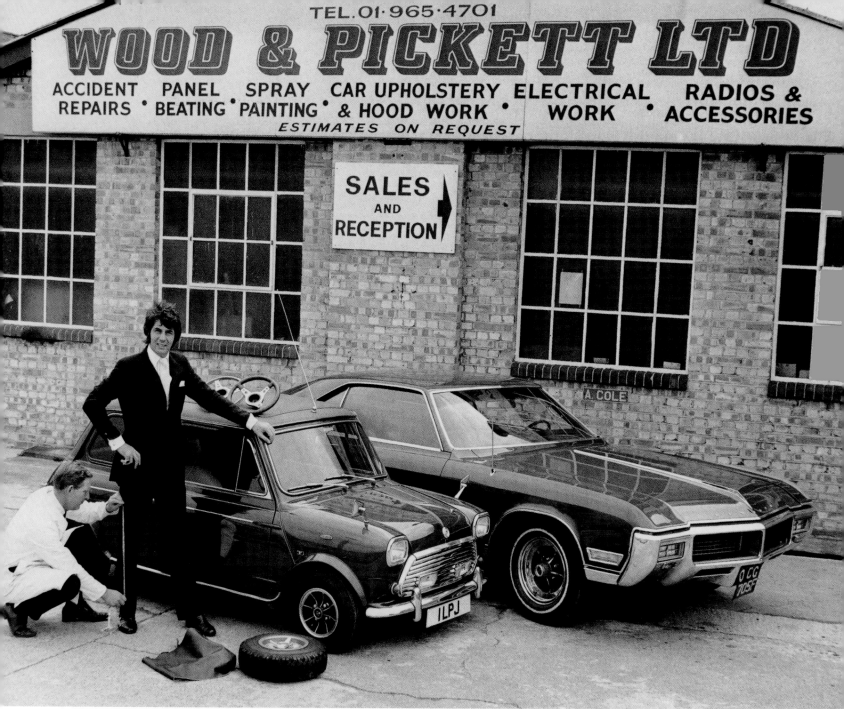

TEL. 01·965·4701

WOOD & PICKETT LTD

ACCIDENT • PANEL • SPRAY • CAR UPHOLSTERY • ELECTRICAL • RADIOS &
REPAIRS • BEATING • PAINTING • & HOOD WORK • WORK • ACCESSORIES

ESTIMATES ON REQUEST

SALES AND RECEPTION

Above Wood & Pickett
could tailor their
Margrave Mini to suit

It transpired that Hooper had some trouble with industrial relations, as all too many firms did in that period of capitalist overburdening and communist undermining. During a strike, two of their men left to set up in business themselves, in a partnership appropriately named Wood & Pickett. Radford was foundering at the time, but Wood & Pickett knew what they were about and took on the titivation of Minis with a zeal that

saw their Margrave Mini come near to being a standard model. Sellers bought one, this time for his partner Britt Eklund. She may or may not have kept it, being like Sellers given to frequent change: the only car she ever fell in love with, to the extent that she sought to buy it back (and succeeded) after disposing of it, was a unique Viotti-bodied Bristol 407 which is still motoring well today.

Left opposite Peter
Sellers and Britt Ekland
with her birthday present
from him, a Radford
Mini de Ville GT
Right Margrave Cooper S
by Wood & Pickett

Left The Margrave interior

So are many sumptuous Minis, all emulating the original Hooper and nearly all making up for the weight of that luxury with the power of a Cooper. Many a firm has gone into the business, and many of those have come out of it again, for it needs craftsmen of sure competence if the work is to be done well; and if it is done badly the result is an unwanted disaster.

That is true of most things; it is particularly true of any modified Mini. The hacksawed convertible, the hackneyed boy-racer, may all too easily bring what was originally right and yare into disrepute. On the other hand, no man has yet made anything that is not susceptible of improvement. Not even the Mini. But any change must delight.

Top and above The Broadspeed Hooligan Mk II. This has a 5-speed gearbox, a 1400 cm³ engine, expert duotone and faded metallic finish, plus unique front and tail styling
Right The Mini Cooper Cabriolet

susceptible of improvement... but change must delight.

'Don't expect me to be modest about the Mini.

I'm very proud that it has run for so long and still

looks like the car we designed.'

SIR ALEC ISSIGONIS

decent

honest

apolitical

Harbinger

advanced

Forty years on, when afar and asunder
Parted are those who are singing today ...

HARROW SCHOOL SONG

The 1960s would have happened here and there and everywhere, with or without the Mini. The little car was not responsible for the redistributions of wealth, of population, of labour, and of social and political influence, that occurred then; nor for the sweeping changes in law, custom, dress, morality, sexual honesty, popular culture, sport, holidaying, commuting, and even in architecture and town planning, that occurred then. It was not responsible for the 1973 oil crisis, nor for consumerism, nor for the conservation, ecology and safety passions which heightened in the period that followed. It is not to be thanked for our freedoms, nor blamed for our failings. All it did was to facilitate all these things. And more.

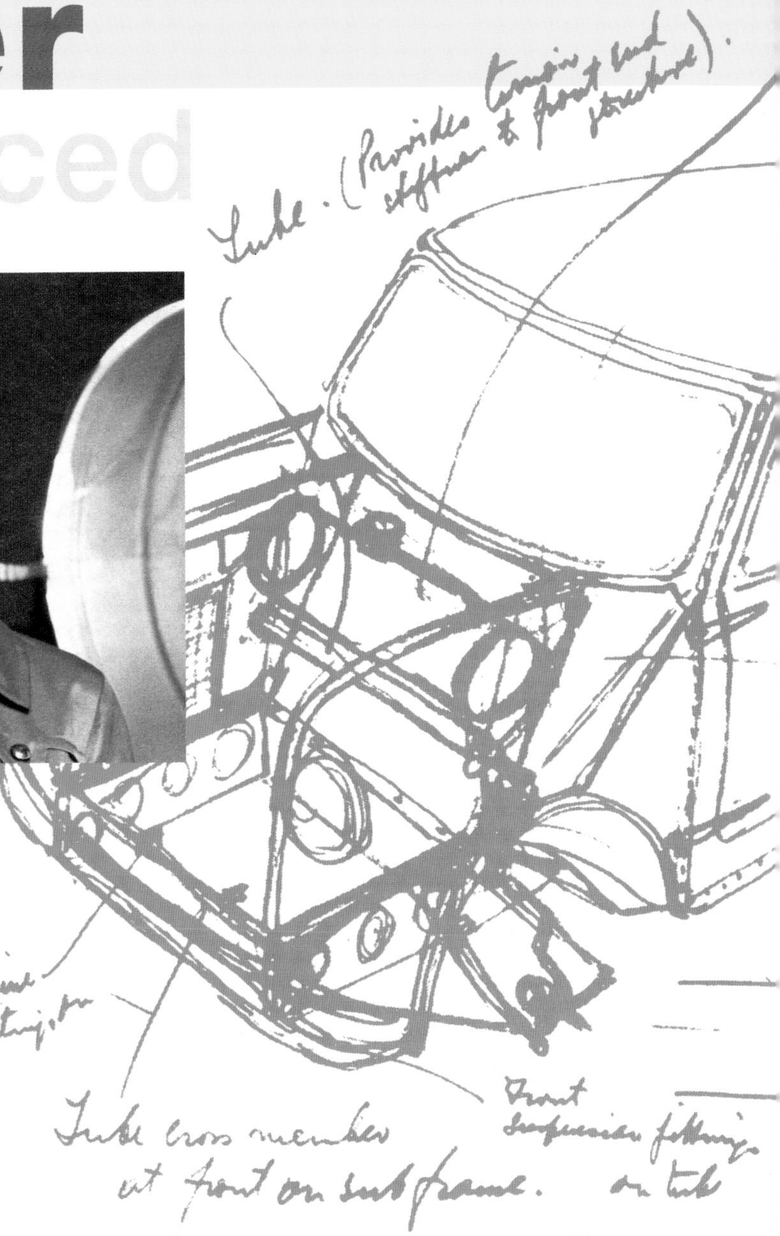

Left 1997 Mini Cooper tail

Light Fifteen

The Mini achieved a revolution in the design and structure of the modern production car. Front-wheel drive was by no means new in 1934 when André Lefebvre, one of the few men in the whole history of the motor industry who deserved to be rated a genius (another was Dr Frederick Lanchester, more than thirty years earlier, and another Alec Issigonis himself), created the celebrated Traction Avant, which we knew in English as the Light Fifteen. That was the car which made front-wheel drive work. The Mini was the car that made it affordable, accessible, scaleable, and fun. All that thereafter remained was for the Fiat to create the 128 and make it

good. It turned up in 1969, resolving all the problems of erratic steering, tricky handling, noise, tyre wear, balance and habitability which had come to the surface in the previous generations. The 128 had modest dimensions, though it was by no means as minute as the Mini; it had brisk performance, decent economy (which still mattered to Europeans), and unprecedented road manners; it also had a transverse engine with an overhead camshaft, a parallel but independently lubricated gearbox, along with radial-ply tyres and several other good things that have since been adopted by every serious maker of popular cars.

Below The Fiat 128, brilliant 1969 model of the modern popular car

Left Mk II Mini;
Mk I blonde

Just as the Pirelli nylon bandage was adopted by
every tyre manufacturer to make the radial-ply
tyre universal, so the engineering refinements of
the Fiat 128 were copied by every manufacturer
of popular cars, which would soon almost
universally take on the front-wheel drive and
transverse-engine layout that the Mini had shown
to be feasible. Yet it was not only the mechanical
refinements of the Fiat which made it the model
for all to copy; there was no less significance in
the fact that, although it had modest dimensions,
it was not as small as the Mini. After a decade,
the Mini had ceased to be the centre of attention,
and Fiat were shrewd enough to see that a car less
obviously extreme (as the Mini still was, if only
dimensionally) would enjoy wider favour.

Below The 1100, elegantly
proportioned bestseller

Below The 1962 Morris 1100

Other manufacturers, notably Ford and Renault, created small front-drive family saloons that were for similar reasons not as small as the Mini. People who were still Mini-minded began to describe these newcomers as the 'super-Mini' class; but they were wrong, quite wrong. There was only ever one true super-Mini: like the Mini *simpliciter*, it came from the pencil of Issigonis and was called the Morris 1100. Never a cult car nor a fashion object, as the Mini had become, the 1100 was wonderfully elegant in its proportions, and was cleverly and sweetly sprung on Dr Moulton's interconnected Hydrolastic (which were never a success beneath the Mini). Few people raved about it (even though Downton

All photos Whatever the age or the guise, the nose or the hinges, any Mini was simply the Mini

made a fully tuned version which was astonishingly quick and competent), but it remained a bestseller in Britain for a remarkably long time. It deserved success everywhere else, too, coming as it did before the Fiat 128; but where else at that time would a buyer give a second thought to anything from the strife-torn British Motor Corporation?

197

The Mini, as always, was an exception; and because its exceptional properties made it a cult car, it could survive against all normal commercial odds. In the 1970s, those odds were stiffening.

Never was there a time when the motor industry was more confused about its choice of direction. Engineering problems could usually be solved, sooner or later; but when those engineering problems were artificial ones thrown up by social caprice, it was hard to know whether or not the cure might be worse than the disease. At that time, current diseases involved war, famine, inflation, pollution, and political ideologies, any one of which was more than any decent self-respecting motor engineer expected to have to redress.

Above Flying the flag in true British Fashion

Above With stars at
the London Palladium,
the 1964 winner of the
Monte Carlo Rally
Right Paddy Hopkirk
shows the showgirls a
thing or two

When the Mini was just five years old, the USA
dropped its pretence of acting as expert advisers
to the anti-communist faction in Vietnam, and the
two sides rushed together into a combat
calculated to prove, by attrition and slaughter,
which was the finer ideology. That war would go
on getting worse and worse for years and years,
and every evening it came home to America on
television. While some of the young men out
there grew more and more vicious and dissolute,
the folks at home felt their anger change to guilt.
Some turned their self-examination to a series of
witch-hunts, the environmentalists and the
safety campaigners joining forces to pillory the
motor industry – while the government, relieved
to see how this counter-irritant distracted the
people from contemplation of more painful but
more distant happenings on the other side of the
Pacific, did everything to encourage them.

Right Less elegant than
the Chrysler Building
in the distance, but
better looking than most
of Manhattan's blocks

Left and below

The Mini range at its most extensive, nothing like the Impala at its most expansive

The American car industry was in effect taken out of the world scene, and the world was shut out of America, as emissions laws starting in California and culminating in the Clean Air Act of 1970 threatened to grow ever more stringent. Never mind that most of the ambient foulness in the air was not the fault of the car; society decreed that the car should put it right. The desperate measures taken in that cause made the American engine ill-mannered and thirsty, while defensive measures to satisfy crash-safety legislation made the rest of the car equally deplorable. In 1970 America built only 6.6 million cars.

In 1965 the figure had been 9,305,561 (and not one of them was remotely like a Mini!), while Japan had made only 696,176, even fewer than Canada. By 1972 Japan's figure was 4.02 million, having passed West Germany the year before to make Japan the world's second largest car maker. Only after the beginning of 1973, when the Vietnam War ended, did the US industry recover and build a record 9.7 million.

By the end of that year, the whole world was in a panic. Having conspicuously failed to defeat Israel in the Yom Kippur war, being instead humiliated in the space of twelve days, the Middle Eastern oil-producers suddenly raised their prices by no less than 70%, and restricted supplies to certain countries who were deemed to have favoured Israel against the Arabs.

This was a threat to the livelihoods of all those in countries dependent on foreign supplies of oil, which included the Americans because they had worked on the basis of conserving their own reserves and buying from abroad. Japan, France and Britain were not the only ones at risk; there was utter panic almost everywhere. For a few months, oil and its products were in desperately short supply, until the markets adjusted to the realization that in fact there was plenty of oil for ages to come and that the shortage was a political artifice. By that time the damage had been done: legislators everywhere, and most wildly in the USA, turned on the motor industry and accused it of being irresponsible in promoting improvident oil consumption. Other industries and services actually used more of it, but it was the car that had to bear the brunt of reducing consumption.

Suddenly it was no longer fashionable – in fact, it was sometimes deemed so antisocial as to be criminal – to drive a big car. Citroën, needing sales to pay for the huge investment in the CX factory, found itself in serious financial trouble and was snapped up by Peugeot. Citroën had belonged to Michelin, but that brave firm which had backed the car maker's engineering audacity for forty years was now as lacking in confidence as all the other tyre companies: supplies of carbon black, and nearly all the synthetic polymers

which had made the modern tyre so much better than the old tree-rubber variety, were derived from petroleum.

Citroën were by no means the only firm in trouble. Volkswagen would have been in trouble anyway, without any oil crisis, having been making the old Beetle for rather too long and finding it hard to adapt to the manufacture of modern cars. The German government had to help; without such assistance, the new Golf (which reached the market in 1974) might never have been born.

The oil crisis had been renamed the Energy Crisis, making the connection easier to see. However, calling it an energy crisis did not persuade governments to ease their pressure on car manufacturers. Far from it: the new and frighteningly stringent regulations about fuel consumption (for example the USA had planned to have everything capable of 27.5mpg by 1985) were superimposed on the recent strictures on emissions and safety, although they were mutually contradictory. The effect was to create a moratorium in car design while every available engineer was put to work sorting out the existing mess. To step out of line was tantamount to suicide: never was there such a display of convergent technology as in the mid-70s, when cars all seemed to become alike and it was very difficult to like any of them. From this time on, the car for the common man served only to make him more common. From this time on, the progress that car engineering made was almost irrelevant to the Mini in particular: it merely applied to all cars in general. From this time on, there was no more scope for individuality until the 80s had succeeded the 70s and almost reached to the 90s.

Right This badge shows how the Mini was integrated into the Rover Group organization in the late 1980s and early 1990s

From this time on, those cars that have been generally successful have all had transverse engines crammed with most of the rest of the necessary machinery into a bonnet lengthened to aid crash-absorption but otherwise as compact as the principles of the Mini dictated. They have had wheels as nearly at the extreme corners of the hull as possible, aiding ingenious and mostly independent suspension systems to provide roadholding and stability as good as a comfortable ride would allow. They have grown wider and lower and shorter than their predecessors, pursuing a trend that the 1934 Citroën Traction suggested and the 1959 Mini confirmed. In their

turn these modern cars have confirmed most of the principles of the Mini, even though the strictures of modern times and marketing methods have prevented them from being strict echoes. In most details, from aerodynamics to ergonomics and from combustion-chamber design to cabin design, they are as naturally superior to the Mini (at a comparable age) as time must dictate, and in most ways they are far less entertaining.

Those cars that were liked most, as the new dawn grew clearer, came from Japan, which was sufficiently free from the constraints of any national tradition to be able to supply whatever

people demanded. Elsewhere, national traditions took many a hard knock: even Italy caught the creeping contagion of speed limits, imposed ostensibly to save fuel but basically because it was a form of regulation that appealed to almost any government anxious to appear to be doing something. In 1975, North Sea oil began to flow into British refineries, but it did little for the British motor industry, which in 1975 produced only 1.2 million cars after expectations of twice that many a couple of years earlier. The American industry was in just as parlous a condition, reduced to an output of 6.7 million just two years after its 9.7 million peak.

Times were hard for everybody. Inflation was rampant all over the world, many parts of which were still suffering from the acute famine which had run like a plague through the previous two or three years. It was not hard to see the link between poverty and hunger, between too little purchasing power and too many mouths to feed: the world population had doubled in 45 years. In the five years from 1970, it had grown by 357 million, and in a few more months it was to reach 4,000 million. It began to be clear that the problem was not too many cars: the problem was too many people.

Above left The making of a Mini: gather all these and…
Above assemble them like that (though you see here a Hydrolastic version)…
Right and this is what you got in rubber-sprung 1959

Above Issigonis

Below The assembly hall

NO SMOKING BEYOND THIS BOARD

About 25 million of these people were working on or with cars. One in every two Americans owned a car, one in every four Britons, one in fifty Peruvians, one in five hundred Indians. Seventy years after Henry Ford had championed the cause of a 'car for the people', there was still some way to go.

Issigonis had meant the Mini to be the definitive step towards that goal. Had all manner of things not happened that did, his aim might have succeeded; but things had to go on in the real world, and any idea that the Mini could serve it as a universal carriage had to be dismissed as a dream beyond hope, as well as beyond avarice. It had become a beloved cult car, and because of that modest service it might endure when all others of its age had gone away.

And yet, and yet ... If there are too many people, and if every one of them may justifiably demand to have a car, seeing that there are as yet few acceptable alternatives, does it not follow that while people have to accept living in more cramped conditions – flats instead of houses, rooms instead of flats, a bed rather than a room – they must also accept that their cars should be smaller than they habitually are? Do we all need full five-seat saloons? With the kerbs crammed, does not the notion of something as short as the Mini (or shorter, even) have a lot to commend it? There are people who see other virtues in the miniaturization of the car. Nothing is more conducive to light weight than small dimensions, and at speeds below the influence of aerodynamics nothing is as beneficial to low fuel consumption as light weight.

Above These Minis featured in the 1998 film, *The Avengers*

There might be other causes for championing the low-mass car: its crash impact, for instance, is proportionately low. So far, the insurance companies of the world have bade us build cars that will not suffer much if they hit something; morality may yet persuade us that it would be more proper to build cars which will not harm much if they hit something. In that case, we may consider the fact that the amount of energy transferred by a 44-ton truck hitting something at 55 mph is so great that a 1-ton car would have to be doing over 364 mph to equal it. If you *must* play 'last across', do it in front of a Mini.

Left and right This beautiful head-turner is a 1997 celebration of the Mini's Monte Carlo Rally hat-trick, 30 years earlier. Known as the ACV30, it is a 'concept car', and led the Monte Carlo Rally winning Minis from 1964, 1965 and 1967 together with their respective drivers, Hopkirk, Makinen and Aaltonen, around the circuit in Monte Carlo in January 1997.

Below Silverstone
celebrates 30 years of
the Mini

Right Minis, led by
Gordon Spice, racing at
Crystal Palace in 1966

Miniaturization has achieved wonders in modern times. In particular, the world of electronics – which has effectively dealt with the pollution crisis and the consumption crisis and with the difficulties of designing cars for safety in crashes, for economy in manufacture, and for reliability on the road – has done wonders in reducing the size of car control systems, as well as in refining their functions and amplifying their scope. Is it possible that miniaturization of the non-habitable part of the car (already down to 20% of the total volume in the Mini, which has yet to be bettered in this respect – or did its big Austin 1800 brother actually do so?) could be carried so much further, until each person's vehicle would occupy little more space than that person? If you must follow some example, is there a better one in this respect than the Mini?

There is nothing so appetizing as pie in the sky. Nor is there anything so foolish as the denial of something that lies in the future beyond our present comprehension. Did the passengers on those noble steam trains of the 1870s envisage the possibility of the self-propelled horseless carriage which we know as the motor car? Did the people making slow furrows on the brow of the sea in the 1890s expect the aeroplane to change travel beyond imagination? Did the artillery officers of the First World War feel threatened by the imminence of the atomic bomb? Could the maker of the first petrol-engined car (he was sixteen years ahead of Benz and Daimler but, being Jewish, his name – Siegfried Markus – was suppressed by Nazi Germany) have envisaged the Mini?

The Mini's illustrious history has seen it carrying out tasks from bringing home the shopping to winning numerous motorsport victories. It has firmly established a strong bond with the British public and, with nearly 5.3 million produced, it is listed in the *Guinness Book of Records* as the most successful British car ever. Today the Mini remains in production with around 15,000 cars rolling off the production line in Longbridge, 60% of which are exported to Japan.

In 1995, a poll organized by *Autocar* voted the Mini the 'Car of the Century'; in 1996, a panel of experts from *Classic and Sportscar* magazine voted the Mini Cooper to be the 'No. 1 Classic Car of All Time'. Indeed, Sir Alec Issigonis' single-mindedness created such a unique car that its personality has continued to shine through four decades of manufacture. Although the casual observer may find the car to appear identical to

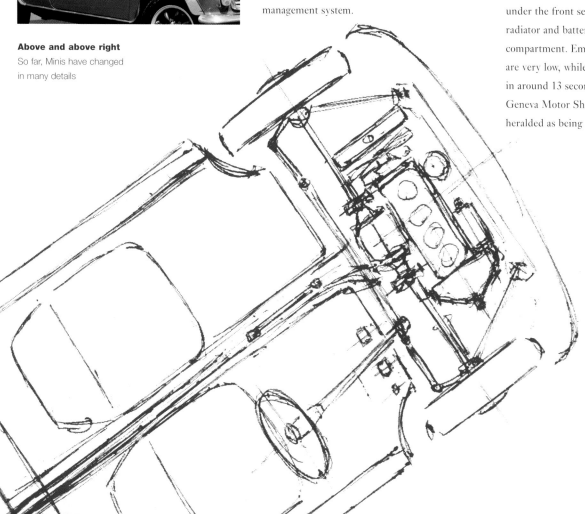

Above and above right
So far, Minis have changed
in many details

the original 1959 model, many developments have taken place under its skin. While these developments began in the 1960s with such alterations as wind-up windows and enclosed door-hinges, 1990s additions have included driver's air-bag, multi-point fuel injection, side impact bars and a sophisticated engine management system.

If there is to be some kindred leap into the future, some new form of private transport some thirty years into the future, its timing will be about right. New safety and environment legislation means things will have to change. The Mini designers are already thinking about and addressing the needs of future generations with the Mini concept cars. The design of the Spiritual is true to the spirit of the Mini, while at the same time, tackling the social and environmental issues of tomorrow. This design concept, weighing only 700 kg, creates a 3.1 m (c. 10 foot), 3-door car with an engineering philosophy which applies an innovative approach to known technology. The flat, 3-cylinder engine is positioned under the rear seat, optimizing safety performance with the firewall-to-front bumper length used for crash management. The fuel tank has been placed under the front seats, while the spare wheel, radiator and battery are situated in the front compartment. Emissions and fuel consumption are very low, while 100 kph can be reached from 0 in around 13 seconds. When launched at the Geneva Motor Show in 1997, the Spiritual was heralded as being far ahead of its time.

Right A more complete
change was visualized
in 1997 in this concept
car, the Spiritual

Left This was the Mini Cooper as you could have bought it, new, in 1998

As always at the end of a century, and even more at the end of a millennium, we tend to look back and think of how well we did certain things, and how good they are. Shortly after the turn of the century and millennium, we shall almost certainly dismiss all that and start to look forward.

With due gratitude to the past in which the Mini never went away, will there be a Mini in that future? Indeed there will. The new Mini is to be launched early in the new millennium. This car will maintain Mini's traditional character while combining it with an advanced engineering design. If it can look backward without feeling retrograde, if it can look forward without seeming rootless, it will surely be welcome. If it is truly a Mini, it will, no less surely, be fun.

A future Mini ?
...indeed there will be.

Above and right Beyond memories of the distant or recent past, is what we have been told would be 'The Car for the 21st Century'

The new Mini 40

GB

'Nought to sixty in a heartbeat and the finest four-wheel drift in Christendom.'

BOB OLIVER

Picture Credits